PASSION TO SERVE, GROW, AND PROSPER

Passion to Serve, Grow, and Prosper

R1 International's Journey to
Become the World's Largest
Rubber Trading Company

Sandana Dass

LIONCREST
PUBLISHING

PASSION TO SERVE, GROW, AND PROSPER
*R1 International's Journey to Become the World's
Largest Rubber Trading Company*

ISBN   978-1-5445-1142-9 *Paperback*
          978-1-5445-1141-2 *Ebook*

To each and every member of the R1 family, past and present, without whose dedication and contribution I could not have developed my ideas about serving and growing a business against the odds, driven by passion

and

To my wife, Anne Debra, and my sons, Joshua Harsha and Juleon Toshan, the love and strength of my life and the inspiration for this book.

Contents

Foreword

BY OEI HONG BIE, CHAIRMAN OF
SINGAPORE TONG TEIK PTE LTD

I've been in the rubber industry for seven decades, since I was eighteen years old. In that time, I've met very few people with the passion to shape their profession and the vision to imagine what is possible. Sandana Dass is one of those rare people.

For me, meeting Sandana was fate—as we Chinese say, *mìngyùn*. The first time we met was more than thirty years ago, in 1986. I was a committee member of the Rubber Association of Singapore, while Sandana was a committee member of the Malaysian Rubber Exchange and Licensing Board (MRELB). We both found ourselves participating in a joint meeting between the Singaporean and Malaysian rubber boards.

Sandana was the youngest person in the meeting, but he never shied away from making a contribution. He participated actively, offering his views on a number of the issues under discussion. Even at such a young age, he stood out from the crowd and showed tremendous potential.

Over the three decades since that first meeting, Sandana has become a visionary in the industry. He can always be relied on to think progressively and express himself with distinction. He is a diligent problem solver determined to create solutions that benefit all parties. During his distinguished career, he has consistently sought new ways to understand the issues facing the rubber industry, offering numerous innovative ideas and approaches.

Perhaps the finest of these came in the year 2000. The rubber business was at a historically low level, to the extent that it was causing major social and political problems in rubber-producing countries. The Malaysian ministers responsible for the rubber industry approached Sandana for advice. The country's farmers were suffering from the low prices and facing extreme poverty.

How did Sandana address the issue? He developed a process whereby the Malaysian government purchased rubber from the farmers at fair market prices. This saved them from desperate poverty and sent the message that there was a guaranteed market for their products. Soon, confidence in the market rose again and prices increased. This idea was subsequently adopted by other rubber-producing countries, such as Thailand and Indonesia.

Sandana's determination once again came to light when he strove to create R1 in 2001. Faced with the challenges of coordinating the efforts of numerous stakeholders, he showed remarkable persistence. At one stage, it appeared that his efforts had failed, but he refused to give up and eventually founded the organization that has become the world's largest international rubber trading company.

On a personal level, I invested $1 million in R1. Including dividends, I have received nearly $9 million in return. Sandana played a leading role in growing the company from the ground up, and it has delivered consistently outstanding returns in a volatile and challenging industry.

Just as importantly, R1 is built on a strong foundation of values and principles. It has defined the rubber industry, leading the way in professionalism, management practices, and risk management. R1 was the first rubber trading company to truly operate globally. Yet the company has always sought to respect the relationship between rubber producers and rubber consumers.

This platform places R1 in an exceptionally strong position to continue evolving with the ever-changing industry. With new majority shareholders, it can develop further and grow even more, while staying close to its founding values.

In a world of instant gratification, Sandana Dass demonstrates what is possible for people who are willing to align themselves to a greater cause and work hard. On both a personal and professional level, he is a remarkable role model, illustrating the value of patience, persistence, and hard work.

Today, there is more than ever a need for people who will refuse to give up when things become difficult, continue to be proactive, and adapt to ever-changing market conditions. As the rubber industry evolves, perhaps this book can play a role in inspiring a new generation of visionary leaders.

SINGAPORE, JULY 17, 2017

Introduction

In 2001, R1 International was founded with initial capital of US $7 million. During the period covered by this book—the company's first fifteen years—that $7 million grew by a factor of more than sixteen, reaching $113.7 million. In that time, R1's total turnover was $18.3 billion, with an average annual turnover of $1.22 billion.

Over the course of a decade and a half, R1 has played a role in the transaction of 17.4 million tons of rubber, with an average of 1.2 million tons of rubber transactions each year. Most impressively, the group has returned an average annual equity of 24 percent to shareholders with a maximum annual return of 49 percent. In a mature commodity industry with low profit margins, these numbers are unprecedented.

Many people want to know how we do this. How is it possible for R1 to consistently achieve returns well above the industry average? I've worked in the rubber trade since 1973. I know that it's an industry with low margins and periods of boom and bust. When R1 was founded, I took it upon myself to redefine what was possible by creating sound processes and intelligent systems, hiring the right people, and building a virtual global company. As I write, R1 operates in nine different countries and twelve locations, yet every employee is linked in real time.

From the company's inception, it was clear that we needed to develop a strong corporate culture to bind together people who work at a distance from one another. I knew that to succeed, we needed to align people in pursuit of a common inspirational vision. From the very beginning, our corporate culture was designed to unite people through shared goals, values, beliefs, and behavior. We sought to inculcate a sense of belonging and teamwork so that we could all move forward in the same direction.

What was the vision? Simply to be number one. We aimed to redefine the industry and become number one in our chosen field. How did we translate this vision into action? We did this through three words: *serve*, *grow*, and *prosper*.

Traders are renowned for having very high opinions of

themselves and preferring to work alone, so it takes something special to unite them into a team. We worked hard to send the message to our traders that R1 is only strong if we work together. The company grew from merging the activities of a Malaysian rubber giant, MARDEC, and Cargill, the largest commodity trader in the United States. Cargill was ready to end its interest in rubber, but with persistence, I convinced the company's leaders to reconsider.

From its inception, the company has always been composed of people from different backgrounds and different countries. At first, there was a lot of cultural conflict, but over time the sense of shared vision, shared mission, and shared process grew strong enough to unite these disparate groups. There's no secret to R1's success. Our competitors could try to copy what we've done. But they probably won't be able to sustain it without the overarching vision that drives us to be number one. Although they may see what is visible, it is unlikely they'll be able to replicate everything that makes R1 special. That takes a commitment to building a unique corporate culture, day by day, over years and decades.

WHY I WROTE THIS BOOK

Sometimes I think I should have written this book a long time ago. The impetus, however, came from a change of shareholders and the realization that, at some point in time, I must step off the bus and pass on the running of R1 to others. I want to leave an internal record for future employees and shareholders, an account of my experiences, and a guide to further success. R1 was built on a desire to create something sustainable and to redefine the rubber industry. This book is an opportunity for me to share the company's story. When the time comes for me to leave the group, I may move into academia or consultancy, and it's my hope that this text can serve as reference material for understanding R1's journey.

Despite founding R1, I never talk about business at home. I have two sons who may one day wish to understand their father's life and achievements. I hope that, if that day comes, this book can also serve as a reference for them. I'd like them to understand the importance of investing in themselves, working hard, and being passionate about what they do. Even when I was a young man, I always wanted to leave behind a legacy. This book is part of that legacy.

CHAPTER ONE

The Seed, the Inspiration, the Destiny

As a boy, I dreamed of becoming a priest. I thought that was how I would save souls. Later, as a young man, I hoped to become a lawyer, defending the poor, the downtrodden, and the victimized. I always believed that my life would be put to some greater purpose.

Eventually, however, I graduated with a degree in economics. This was in 1973. At the time, there was only one university in Malaysia. Today, there are more than seventy. With so few spaces available, I had to fight for my place at university. When I graduated, I knew—like everyone else in my position—that the world was at my feet. I could choose any career I wanted. My friends chose to enter the civil service, become experts in foreign affairs, or move into trade counseling. These were glamorous roles. I wanted to choose a career where I could do maximum good while also earning a good living. Deep in my heart, I wanted both to do well and to do good.

It was in this frame of mind that I saw an advertisement for a year's scholarship in rubber marketing with the Malaysian Rubber Fund Board. In 1973, Malaysia was a developing country. The economy was largely based on agriculture, and rubber was a major bedrock, contributing substantially to GDP. More than half a million rubber farmers depended on rubber for their livelihoods.

I'd taken classes in rural economics, and I knew from my degree that these farmers were exploited and manipulated by the middlemen to whom they sold their rubber, leaving the farmers with such meager incomes that they were classified as living below the poverty line. When I saw the advertisement for the year's scholarship in rubber marketing, I realized that it was an opportunity to positively impact the lives of many small farmers. I applied and became one of only three people to receive the scholarship.

The purpose of the rubber scholarship was to select and train capable young men, with the goal of placing them in a dedicated government agency which looks after the interests of smallholders. They were to be tasked with promoting and selling rubber, grown by smallholders and processed by central rubber factories, directly to customers worldwide. The aim of the initiative was to bring the rubber produced by smallholders directly to the doorsteps of consumers throughout the globe. The board hoped that this dedicated and innovative marketing channel would boost the incomes of farmers in the country.

The program was an intense learning experience. The first few months took place in the rubber factories of Malaysia, where I learned about factory operations, sourcing, machinery, different types of rubber, and everything else I needed to know about the Malaysian side of the industry. I benefited hugely from the experience of immersion into rubber processing. Today, many young people working in the trade rarely experience the realities of factory life. Yet I can still recall the sights, sounds, and smells I experienced while living and working in the factory. It was then, I think, that the plight of smallholders and the enormous potential of rubber truly entered my heart.

Following that experience, the next phase of the training took me to London and a few other European cities so that I could learn the basics of marketing and trading rubber. It was my first time traveling outside of Malaysia, a time of both excitement and trepidation. In Britain, I met many rubber scientists who were manufacturing and testing a range of rubber products. That gave me exposure to the different ways in which raw rubber was converted into manufactured products. For example, I witnessed the manufacture of tires, technical and engineered rubber goods, foam mattresses, catheters, and gloves. My instructors—including Graham Drake, Tom Pendle, K. F. Heinisch, and Hon Kok Kee—explained how the intrinsic properties of rubber applied to the production of different types of rubber goods.

Next, I embarked on various short attachments with the technical and advisory bureau of the Malaysian Rubber Fund Board. There, I learned from rubber consumers such as Pirelli and Continental. I was a young man, directly out of university and privileged to mix with people who were important in the rubber industry. Their passion and dedication touched me and inspired me to emulate them. They loved what they were doing, and that transmitted to me and made me want to contribute to the industry.

In addition to these technical attachments, I spent time with the foremost rubber trading companies in London, Paris, and Hamburg. These included Pacol; Czarnkow; Lewis & Peat; Hecht Heyworth & Alcan; Safic-Alcan; and Nordmann, Rassmann. As you might imagine, I learned an enormous amount about the rubber trade and the operation of rubber markets during these sojourns.

I loved to listen to the stories, told by experienced traders, of how markets and prices moved. They conveyed an impression that the industry was exotic, exhilarating, and mystifying. I was fascinated by—even in awe of—the knowledge and passion of these experienced super traders and marketers. It seemed to me that the actions of these few people could influence—positively or negatively—the livelihood of rubber smallholders worldwide.

Meeting these leaders and learning from them in person was a rare privilege. Their passion for their work was both inspiring and infectious, and I felt exceptionally fortunate to be in such company. Additionally, I realized that, with the right motivation and a good sense of timing, I too could make a big difference. Even today, I can easily recall the names of the prominent traders who generously shared their experience and advice with me, particularly Arnost Propper of Pacol, Roy Windsor of Czarnkow, David Beech of Hecht Heyworth & Alcan, Eduard Nordmann from Nordmann, Rassmann, and Alain Alcan of Safic-Alcan.

The knowledge I gained during my time in the UK, Italy, France, Germany, and Austria formed a solid foundation on which I would build for the rest of my career.

When I returned to Malaysia, however, I had a more immediate decision to make. Where would I begin my career? I had the alluring opportunity to take up a position with the Malayan Rubber Fund Board. To a young man from a humble background, their sparkling, modern office building, strategically located in the center of Kuala Lumpur, was dazzling. The main foyer contained a beautiful fountain, a sight I had never before seen. Additionally, the board's employees, from diverse backgrounds and cultures, were extremely friendly and helpful. Even the staff canteen, offering a sumptuous selection of meals, was appealing. I was naturally tempted by all these attractions, and almost made the decision to join the company.

A PASSION TO SERVE

Destiny however, decreed differently. By chance, while I was visiting the office of the Malaysian Rubber Fund Board, I happened to meet an Englishman named John Morris, who served as the general manager of the Malaysian Rubber Development Corporation (MRDC, later renamed MARDEC). The company's role was to assist smallholders in the task of upgrading the quality of their raw materials and attaining fair prices.

John invited me to come to his house, so that he could explain the work of MRDC. I accepted and, when I arrived, he offered me a glass of beer. I grew up in a family where no one drank alcohol, but I wanted to be polite to my new business acquaintance, so I accepted gratefully. Seeing John gulp his drink in one draught, I assumed this was the appropriate way to consume beer and followed suit. As a first-time drinker, this had a powerful impact on my system and, to my lasting embarrassment, I soon felt sick and threw up right in front of my host!

Fortunately, John was exceptionally gracious and understanding. He overlooked my indiscretion and invited me to join him the next morning for a tour of MRDC rubber factories in Negeri Sembilan and Malacca and a continuation of our discussion. Gladly, I accepted. It was an experience that shaped the path of my life.

John was an extraordinary man. That day when I went with him to visit MRDC's factories, he drove approximately three hundred kilometers. In his company, I saw the lives of farmers firsthand. They showered me with warmth and kindness, and I saw the problems they faced. They were exploited by mid-level dealers, to whom they lived in constant debt. Their lives were a cycle of poverty. Previously, I had understood the economic foundations of the industry, but it was only when I visited the farmers with John that I saw for myself the challenges the farmers faced. Meeting them and seeing their struggles for myself touched my heart.

I always knew that I wanted to be of service. It was only when I met John and visited the factories of MRDC that I understood exactly how. My internal desire met an external need that I was uniquely qualified to serve. I grew up with a strong Christian background. As a young man, I was idealistic and had an interest in socialism. My family was also in business, so business was in my blood. My faith, my political leanings, and my business acumen, combined with the passion inspired by my meetings with poor farmers, fired me into action.

Before we parted company, John Morris invited me to join MRDC. I said yes and started the next day. I stayed with the company for twenty-eight years, until 2001.

A TRANSFORMING INDUSTRY

My twenty-eight years at MRDC/MARDEC saw me rise from marketing officer to director of marketing, to director of operations/joint ventures, and I eventually became the managing director of MARDEC International. At the start of my career, MRDC was a government organization. By the time I left the company, it had been privatized and I was a management shareholder, albeit with a very minor stake. From 2004 until 2012, I served as a nonexecutive director on the MARDEC board. As you might imagine, I saw many changes in the Malaysian rubber industry during my career.

Prior to the early 1970s, rubber was often produced by hand, graded visually, and shipped in the form of bales. During my tenure with MARDEC, the process was already transforming. Rubber was manufactured as a raw material in central processing factories to technical specifications. This made it possible to consistently produce high-quality rubber, which was then packed into pallets and shipped.

MARDEC had fifteen factories located around the country, which together processed 14 percent of the rubber produced by Malaysian smallholders. During the early days of the transformation, which was known as the Standard Malaysian Rubber Scheme, MARDEC was responsible for sourcing, processing, and marketing rubber from smallholders to consumers all over the world. In collaboration with the Rubber Fund Board and the Ministry for Primary Industries, I was fortunate to be a part of this mission.

At the time, 80 percent of world rubber consumption took place in industrialized countries such as European nations, Japan, and the United States. Naturally, with such a large market on their doorstep, most rubber trading companies were also based in these countries. The world centers of rubber trading were in London and New York. We wanted to promote our new form of rubber and sell it directly to consumers all over the world. We wished to convince customers to buy from MARDEC directly, bypassing the trading houses.

This role led me to travel for six months of the year during my first ten years with the company, a period during which I took hardly any holidays. By the end of that decade, I had traveled the world numerous times and visited almost seventy countries in Western and Eastern Europe, the United States, Canada, Central America, South America, and Asia.

While this was hard work, it was also an enormous privilege. I got to know the industry and interact with people from many different cultures, all in the service of promoting and selling rubber produced by Malaysian smallholders. I met leaders of tire and rubber goods factories, trading companies, and futures exchanges in Chicago, New York, and Tokyo. I even led negotiation of the first long-term rubber contract between the government of Malaysia and the government of Brazil, ironically the country where natural rubber was originally cultivated.

Looking back, I see how that period of my life shaped my outlook on the world, and ultimately contributed to the creation of R1. Sometimes I meet young people who prefer to stay in their comfort zone, and who avoid moving to unfamiliar countries and experiencing new cultural milieus. Yet I believe it's one of the most import-ant experiences a person who wishes to succeed can have. Travel helped me to develop empathy, curiosity, and cour-age, all qualities that have served me well since then. For example, meeting so many prestigious people and speak-ing to different leaders gave me the confidence to speak to anyone, no matter how lofty their position. In summary, my years of travel instilled in me a global outlook which positively shaped my view of work, people, and life.

Nonetheless, I always remembered that I traveled as a rep-resentative of both MARDEC and Malaysia. I took pride in conveying to consumers the fact that the rubber we offered was produced directly by farmers in central factories. Prior to my advocacy, many of the people I spoke to weren't aware that their rubber came from Malaysia. Today, many large consumers of rubber buy directly from producers, but in the 1970s, the situation was very different. They dealt primarily with big trading houses in London and New York, so they didn't consider the possibility that the rubber they purchased originated somewhere else.

It took a lot of work to persuade them to change their habits. I urged major consumers such as Firestone, Uniroyal, Goodyear, Pirelli, and Continental to see buying from MRDC as a form of corporate social respon-sibility (CSR). When they purchased from MRDC, they were serving rubber smallholders.

Later, in the 1990s, Malaysia moved from agriculture toward industrialization. I was responsible for encouraging investment, and I sought out an opportunity for international rubber-product manufacturers to relocate their factories to Malaysia, where they could be close to the source of rubber production. We brought in a broad range of manufacturers, including makers of latex thread and hydraulic rubber hoses from Italy, a balloon manufacturer from the United Kingdom, and a glove manufacturer from Australia. It was a move that brought benefits to both sides.

In recent years, there has been a huge migration of the rubber industry toward Asia. In the 1970s, 80 percent of rubber worldwide was consumed in the developed countries of the West. Since then, however, the economies of China and India have developed hugely. In 2018, approximately 70 percent of the world's rubber will be consumed in Asia. Malaysia, the most iconic rubber producer on the planet, is no longer the world's largest producer. Over the years, the country has moved toward palm oil and other industries, diminishing the importance of rubber. It is this shift that led me to create a rubber company with a global focus.

A CRISIS AND A CONTRIBUTION

Over the course of my years with MARDEC, the rubber

industry naturally went through many highs and lows. Like any commodity, rubber experiences periods of boom and bust. At times, prices were extremely low, causing small farmers severe hardship. Since the 1920s, various governments and international organizations had attempted to control and manage rubber prices, but all their efforts ended in failure. At times, the Malaysian government sought to assist farmers by artificially lifting rubber prices. While their intentions were good, it's not possible for governments to intervene arbitrarily in markets and push up rubber prices in a free global market.

In 1999, rubber prices dropped through the floor. The price, which stood at 495 Malaysian sen per kilo in 1995, had collapsed to 195 sen per kilo by early 1999—a staggering 60 percent decline in prices in the space of less than four years. At the time, I was part of a group of industry experts responsible for advising Tun Lim Keng Yaik, a Malaysian minister who oversaw the nation's primary industries, including rubber. We spoke regularly, discussing the state of the rubber market.

On one occasion, he called me from Parliament House to tell me that farmers were agitating for higher rubber prices. With prices at historic lows, farmers could barely feed their families, and the prime minister was extremely concerned. The minister's first impulse was to do whatever he could to immediately increase rubber prices.

Unfortunately, as I explained to him, rubber is an international commodity. It's simply not possible to unilaterally increase the price. When he explained that the farmers were ready to protest, I said that I'd investigate the situation and determine the real issue. I soon discovered that conditions were even worse than we had realized.

We knew that farmers were suffering due to the low prices. What we had failed to understand was that the low prices were leading to an overall loss of confidence in the industry. Factories that were previously reliable buyers of rubber had become extremely cautious and had substantially reduced or halted their purchases; therefore, farmers were not merely suffering from reduced income. They were suffering from a total cessation of their income. They were unable to sell their raw material.

This was alarming, but it was easier to address than low global prices. I formulated and presented a program in which the government and private factories became willing buyers of raw material at market prices—not inflated prices—from smallholders. This gave the farmers a continuing outlet for their produce and provided them with much-needed income. The program was even more successful than I had anticipated.

Farm gate rubber prices, which had been hovering between 92 sen and 120 sen in depressed areas prior to the program, shot up to 140 sen per kilo by the end of the program's first day of operation. In the most depressed areas, this constituted an instantaneous rise of 52 percent. Once we were able to assure farmers that their produce would be purchased, industry confidence rose, and soon the scheme did its work. A normal rubber market was restored.

I consider the opportunity to create this kind of change to be a blessing. Rubber farmers in many countries—not only Malaysia—were facing severe hardship at the time. When rubber prices stabilized and started to increase, producers in Thailand, Indonesia, and other countries also benefited. Naturally, the minister was very happy, and I look back upon that time with great satisfaction, knowing that I was able to make a contribution to the lives and livelihoods of thousands of smallholders. The government recognized me for meritorious service to the country and, in 2001, His Majesty the King of Malaysia conferred on me the prestigious title of Darjah Johan Mangku Negara (JMN), or the Most Esteemed Order of the Defender of the Realm.

DO GOOD, DO WELL

I'm a businessman, but I also believe very strongly that each one of us is here to make a unique contribution in the world. The love that inspires us, the people around us, and the convictions we form in our hearts shape our ability to serve. Life may give us challenges and tribulations, but we must always nurture the desire to do good as we do well. Without these guiding principles, it's impossible to imagine that I would have built R1 on strong foundations.

I look around today and see many people seeking instant gratification. They are impatient and hurried. Yet I believe that for our lives to have meaning, we must have a purpose. We must be willing to make sacrifices. We must have the patience, determination, and grit to face many challenges. This is especially true in the rubber industry, which is a mature industry requiring investment and persistence. With these qualities, we can build a strong foundation and contribute to the betterment of the lives of others.

In the following chapter, I'll share the story of how I came to found R1, the company that has become the vehicle for so many of my own contributions in this life.

CHAPTER TWO

From Dream to Vision

Until 1991, Malaysia was the largest producer of rubber in the world, with the country accounting for nearly 38 percent of total global production. In the early 1990s, however, the industry peaked and began to decline. For those of us working in the industry, it was clear that the downturn was indicative of a larger trend.

The Malaysian economy was going through a phase of major development. The country was aiming to transition from an agricultural economy into one based more on industry and services. Meanwhile, rubber, the staple of Malaysia's economy, was under threat from newer crops, such as palm oil. When the tide started to turn in the early 1990s, I saw the writing on the wall. Despite seventy-five years as the world leader in rubber production, there was a risk that all the country's accumulated experience—and the respect accrued from being a market leader for many decades—would become obsolete. As our production decreased, so did our reputation in the global rubber trade.

I didn't want to stand by and watch this happen. I knew there was a risk that if the leaders in the Malaysian rubber industry didn't take decisive action, we would lose our preeminent status, and perhaps ultimately be pushed out of the space altogether.

In 1996, this situation led me to approach MARDEC's board of directors. I talked to them about our changing times, and about how we were losing so much more than just our dominant position in the market—we were also losing part of our strength as a nation. I tried to impress upon them the importance of seeking out other opportunities to grow.

My proposal at the time was that we should move offshore and form a global trading company. Unfortunately, these ideas fell upon deaf ears. The board was composed of directors nominated by the Malaysian government. They operated with a highly nationalistic mentality and felt strongly that our business should remain within the borders of the country. At the time, Malaysia was attracting a lot of foreign investment in industry. As a whole, the country was focused on promoting its skilled, low-cost manpower and potential as a venue for import substitution. Most companies, including MARDEC, were afraid to venture offshore. Although I brought up the subject several times, the directors of MARDEC were unwilling to consider the possibility of founding a company that wasn't based in Malaysia.

Nonetheless, I continued to observe the changing economy. In the consumer arena, for example, tire manufacturers were involved in aggressive mergers and acquisitions. Most of the rubber in the world is consumed by fewer than ten tire manufacturers. As the tire industry consolidated in the latter part of the decade, rubber prices collapsed to historic lows. Farmers, faced with a dire loss of income, were driven to protest. In turn, these protests generated political conflict in all the major rubber-producing countries.

In the midst of all this turmoil, I spied an opportunity.

THE SEEDS OF R1

Cargill, based in Minneapolis, is the largest family-owned commodity trading company in the United States. The company was founded in 1865 to trade in the grain market. By 2000, it played a role in the trade of 30 percent of the world's grains and oilseeds.

In 1997, Cargill commissioned the consulting firm McKinsey & Company to study how the company could rationalize its operations. This study recommended that Cargill should make food the company's core business sector. This involved divesting itself of other non-core business—those in which the company wasn't invested in the full value chain—over the following five years. Non-core businesses included any fields in which Cargill didn't have a stake in growing or producing the relevant goods, such as coffee, steel, and—of course—rubber.

At the time, Cargill Asia Pacific was headquartered in Singapore. The organization was involved in trading various origins and grades of rubber, along with numerous other commodities and services. So when I found out the company was planning to close its rubber trading division, I decided the time was right to approach the board with my idea. Instead of closing its rubber division, I proposed that Cargill merge operations with MARDEC, creating a unique global rubber trading conglomerate.

At this time—in 1999—Cargill was an enormous company, operating in fifty-nine countries and employing 82,000 people around the world. The group's annual turnover was in the region of US $50 billion.

I met with Cargill's vice president in Minneapolis, and he agreed that my idea made sense. It would allow the company to keep its rubber trading division open in a way that suited the business demands of a new millennium. At a time when many companies were making members of staff redundant, it would also prevent Cargill from needing to close its Singapore business, so it was both a business opportunity and a positive move for the company's public profile. In July of 2000, Cargill and I drew up a letter of intent and I returned to MARDEC. I informed MARDEC about the opportunity and provided the company with a detailed plan of the business concept.

R1 Business System Concept

R1 core activities (including joint venture supply agreements)

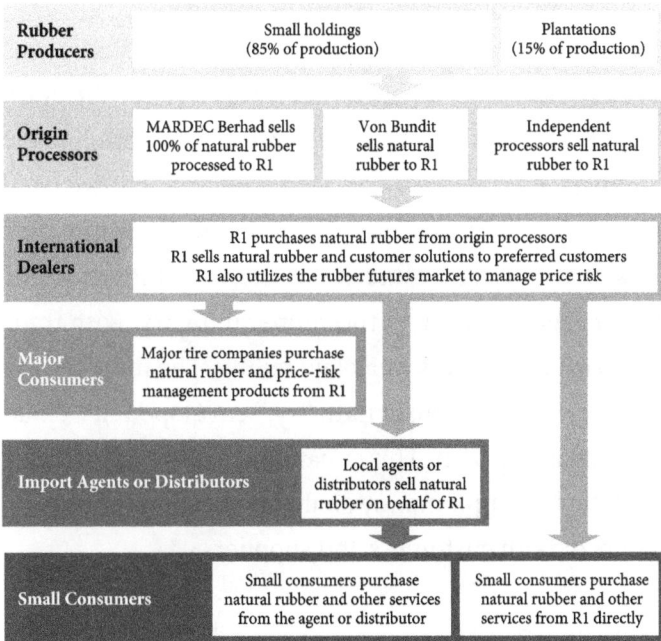

Rubber Producers	Small holdings (85% of production)		Plantations (15% of production)
Origin Processors	MARDEC Berhad sells 100% of natural rubber processed to R1	Von Bundit sells natural rubber to R1	Independent processors sell natural rubber to R1
International Dealers	R1 purchases natural rubber from origin processors R1 sells natural rubber and customer solutions to preferred customers R1 also utilizes the rubber futures market to manage price risk		
Major Consumers	Major tire companies purchase natural rubber and price-risk management products from R1		
Import Agents or Distributors	Local agents or distributors sell natural rubber on behalf of R1		
Small Consumers	Small consumers purchase natural rubber and other services from the agent or distributor		Small consumers purchase natural rubber and other services from R1 directly

As I explained to the board, MARDEC's strength lay in processing, while Cargill was a global trader. As the dynamics of the global rubber trade shifted, it made sense to form a new entity which could compete in this new world. As I envisaged it, this union would give birth to a new, unique global rubber trading company that combined the capabilities of the producer, processor, global trader, and risk manager to achieve synergies and offer increased value. Our products would be better, as would the services and solutions we could offer buyers and suppliers. Additionally, we had a chance to claim an early mover advantage. As the first company of this type, if we succeeded we would likely grow to become the biggest.

I felt too that the timing was right. The industry was already changing so much that it was ripe for the entry of a new kind of player. When creating something new, timing is essential. We can ready the ship, but we need the wind behind us. The opportunity to enter into partnership with Cargill came at a highly opportune moment. There was a vacuum in the rubber industry, with traditional rubber dealers weak and failing. The industry as a whole felt like a "sunset industry," enveloped in a cloud of doom and gloom. This situation created a gap which a credible trading company could fill, meeting the requirements of both customers and suppliers.

At MARDEC, rubber was our only product. As Malaysia's

rubber production continued to drop, we were destined to lose volume and shrink as a company. If production dropped below a certain level, we would face an uneconomical business model, perhaps even oblivion.

It's famously said that if a frog sits in a saucepan of gradually warming water, it won't jump out when the water starts to become uncomfortably hot. It will stay exactly where it is, eventually boiling to death. In the early 2000s, MARDEC was like that frog. If we didn't jump out of a market that was becoming increasingly painful, we would eventually suffer severe injuries. Perhaps the company would even cease to exist.

I emphasized all of this to the board members of MARDEC. Our strategy for success in the new rubber market had to include generating enough volume to sustain the production arm of the business, while finding other ways to maximize value creation. A partnership with Cargill would enable us to achieve economies of scale by increasing our size and efficiency. Through combining the processing, trading, and risk management capabilities of the two companies, we could seek opportunities to leverage our returns, adopting new strategies and increasing our use of the global futures market, a new arena for MARDEC.

In summary, combining our assets was a way to improve

the market position of both companies. It also gave us an opportunity to develop more niche-market product services to cater to the requirements of the marketplace. The new structure would also enable us to develop long-term, trusting partnerships with both customers and suppliers. This heralded a move away from the transactional mindset and toward a desire to create strategic partnerships. It made sense for everyone involved, and I was confident that we were finally moving smoothly toward the creation of a new company. How wrong I was.

HOW R1 TOOK ROOT

Bringing R1 to life was not an easy process. It was important that every company with a stake in the new firm felt that their interests were represented. Moreover, it was vitally important that all partners agreed on certain key issues that would make or break the partnership—and the business. It was essential for R1 to be accepted by customers and producers worldwide as a credible, professional, independent global company, a point on which it was relatively easy to find agreement. Second, and more challenging, I felt it was vital to establish R1 in a neutral location, a move that would make it possible to attract a diverse group of stakeholders from the rubber industry, including professionals, bankers, and support operatives. Singapore was my preferred location.

Why? At the time, all the major rubber procurement offices of the primary tire manufacturers were based in Singapore, meaning that they all made purchases there despite the fact that materials came from Thailand, Malaysia, Indonesia, and any number of other countries. Compounding these advantages, a large number of rubber processors also operated in Singapore, and it already had a recognized rubber futures exchange. In addition, Singapore was already a well-recognized global rubber trading hub, handling almost 70 percent of world rubber trade flow. With all the established infrastructure necessary to trade finance and logistics, Singapore would be an excellent place to base R1.

MARDEC shareholders resisted this idea, however. Although they supported the project, they insisted that R1 must be based in Kuala Lumpur, in accordance with their nationalist ideals about the importance of keeping Malaysian business in Malaysia.

Once again, I had hit a wall. I couldn't convince the board of MARDEC to support my plans to locate the business in Singapore and I was unwilling to move forward with the project until this key condition was met. Fortunately, however, during this time I was an advisor to the government minister in charge of the rubber industry, Tun Lim Keng Yaik. I leveraged this opportunity by meeting with him and explaining my ambitions. I told him why I wanted to form R1, covering the state of the industry, the current situation in Malaysia, and the board's reaction.

The minister was very intelligent, with great business sense. He understood both my perspective and the view of the government officials. After all, he was a politician. The minister spoke to the prime minister and told him the story, describing the great benefits that would accrue to the country as a whole, even if R1 was headquartered in Singapore. Eventually, the prime minister agreed with him, and the minister returned to the board of MARDEC and asked them to reconsider their stance on the location.

Even after reviewing the conditions, the board still refused to budge. Nonetheless, the CEO of MARDEC was a staunch believer in the project and its value to MARDEC. He shared my desire to see MARDEC take off and stood steadfastly by my side. To break this impasse, we proposed another option. We would register the company offshore on the island of Labuan, a Malaysian free-trade investment center, but the operating headquarters would be located in Singapore.

By this time, despite some residual resistance, the board could not say no. On March 30, 2001, they finally compromised and agreed to our plan, albeit with the stipulation that they would only take 45 percent equity in the company. The board of Cargill had already agreed to a stake of 30 percent, with an irrevocable put option to MARDEC in the shareholders' agreement. This guaranteed Cargill that, two years from the formation of R1, it would have the option to sell its stake to MARDEC. If Cargill chose to take up this option, MARDEC would not be able to refuse.

In an effort to protect itself from excessive liability, MARDEC insisted that, in the event of Cargill exercising its put option, I would personally purchase a 14 percent stake in R1—a put and call option. I was confident that R1 would succeed and I understood that, as the founder, I had a responsibility to demonstrate this confidence, so I agreed to MARDEC's condition in the event that Cargill chose to exercise its put option.

Once these agreements had been hammered out, I still needed shareholders willing to take 25 percent equity. After MARDEC Malaysia and Cargill Asia Pacific, I wanted to engage partners from other major rubber-producing countries, such as Thailand and Indonesia. I approached the biggest rubber processing group in Thailand, Von Bundit, which was owned by Thaveesak Holdings and led by Dr. Pongsak Kerdvongbundit. The group operated four processing factories, employed two thousand employees, and was well recognized by the global rubber industry. I approached them as a friend, looking for a partner in the potentially lucrative project I was working to get off the ground.

I also approached the largest Indonesian rubber trader, Kian In Ltd, owned by Oei Hong Bie, the doyen of the rubber trade. I deliberately chose these two companies because they were the top two rubber-producing and trading companies in the world, because of their location, and because of my friendship with them. Neither felt the need to undertake a detailed review of the business plan that I presented to them. Instead, they simply asked, "What percentage do you want us to take?" Thaveesak Holdings took the 10 percent I requested, and Kian In Ltd the remaining 15 percent. And there we had it—a full 100 percent equity secured in what would become R1.

From early 2000 to March 2001, I had overcome countless hurdles and challenges to make R1 a reality. When everything finally fell into place, I was elated—and validated. It would have been easy to give up along the way, but I followed through with this project because I wholeheartedly believed in it, and I was thrilled to see it taking shape. Little did I know that I had another shock in store for me.

SHOCK AND RELIEF

I returned to the Asia Pacific offices of Cargill, excited to share the news that an agreement had been reached with MARDEC and our other partners. The company's representative showed me into the office, sat me down, and promptly dropped a bombshell. He told me that Cargill was dropping out of the partnership discussions. He gave me no reason for this decision. As I left the office and walked back to my hotel, I was shocked, confused, and miserable, with many painful questions running through my mind. What would I say to MARDEC? What would I say to Kian In and to Thaveesak Holdings?

That night I walked the streets of Singapore, poring over my experience of the previous few months. I looked for missteps and mistakes, attempting to resolve my confusion and understand what had happened. After a while, I realized something didn't add up. The entire time I'd been in talks with Cargill, I had dealt with two people: the president and the controller of Cargill Asia Pacific, Rob McRae and Jeral D'Souza. Both had been highly cooperative, supportive, and positive about the partnership. It simply didn't make sense that, with the deal close to completion, someone new would take over from them and inform me that the deal was off.

I called Jeral and told him about the message I'd received, only to discover that he was as surprised as I was. He was traveling back to Singapore that night, so he asked me to stay an extra night and meet him at the Cargill office the following day. Naturally, I agreed.

The next morning, I returned to the office to meet Jeral.

After listening to what I had to say, he made a call to Minneapolis and soon the project was saved. It felt like a miracle. As I discovered, Cargill's financial year ends in May. At the time, it was the end of March and Cargill had not received a response from MARDEC, so Cargill somehow concluded that the deal was dead. It needed to cement the partnership by the end of its financial year, and from its perspective it seemed that MARDEC wasn't moving fast enough.

Compounding this problem, both Jeral and Rob were traveling overseas at the crucial moment when I met with Cargill's representative, who had never supported the project. He was delighted to tell me that Cargill was out. Fortunately, speaking to Jeral relieved my confusion, and he was keen to ensure that we could close the deal before the end of Cargill's financial year.

After returning to Malaysia, I worked as hard as I could to complete the shareholders' agreement and present it to all the relevant parties. On May 24, days before Cargill's year ended, we signed. R1 was born. After twenty-eight years at MARDEC, I faced a new challenge. With the creation of R1, I had to step up and become the leader of a new, unique pure rubber trading company.

Among other changes, this meant moving to Singapore. This was a huge sacrifice for my young family. We had recently moved into our newly constructed dream villa in Kuala Lumpur and my two baby sons—both under the age of three at the time—loved playing in the landscaped garden and the pool. The villa had taken more than two years to build and was situated in a beautiful forested area, overlooking a golf course. To make matters even more complicated, I hadn't discussed the move with my wife. I approached her only when the deal was done, hoping that I could persuade her that moving to Singapore was the right move for us. Fortunately, her support was unwavering. She agreed to the move. With excitement and determination, I could look forward to making a success of a new company, a new challenge, and a new legacy.

In business, simply sustaining the status quo is not an option that leads to lasting success. Getting ahead—and staying ahead—requires foresight and vision. Those who are most successful are those who can read the environment within their industries and position themselves to ride the coming wave, not only the existing one. Leaders rise to the need, seize the moment, maximize their capabilities, and redefine the market. This is how they remain relevant and sustainable.

The business climate is subject to constant change. True leaders understand this, pursuing continuous improvement and weathering transformational changes within their chosen industry. This is the difference between managers and leaders. Sometimes, organizations make the mistake of assuming that an excellent manager will also be an excellent leader, but the two skillsets are very different. Business leaders must be visionaries. The success that I've achieved with R1 is based on this capacity to look ahead and position the company in the right direction. The next chapter will focus more clearly on the qualities of leaders and on the process that brought R1's vision and mission statement to life.

CHAPTER THREE

Serving as a Leader

One of the key traits of a leader is clarity. Leaders who don't understand their goals cannot hope to achieve them. From the foundation of R1, we knew what we wanted to do. We aspired to establish a unique rubber trading company, to redefine the rubber industry, and to become the number one rubber trader in the world. Only when we knew where we wanted to go could we determine which road to take, which vehicle to travel in, which people to employ, and which resources to utilize. This illustrates another key principle of success in business—and in life: begin with the end in mind.

As I reflected on the name for this new partnership, I wanted to choose one that emphasized the goal of becoming number one in the industry, as a way to keep our intentions at the forefront of the business. Eventually, with the assistance of a PR consultant, we arrived at the name R1 International. It embodied our goals without being too obvious: "R" doesn't specifically say "rubber," but when someone sees the name, they know we have something big in mind. I can hand someone a business card and know that the recipient will be curious; if they want to understand the business, they will need to ask me questions. When they do, I have a chance to explain what we do and why.

Battles are won in the mind before we even enter the field. To achieve our goals, we must visualize every step along the way. At R1, we determined that we would become the number one global rubber trader and that decision informed all of our choices.

To accomplish this goal, our partnership with Cargill was particularly beneficial. One of the main benefits was the firm's existing global trading presence. Initially, Cargill helped us to establish systems of trading, operations, risk management, credit control, and finance—the value I knew they would provide when I first sought to forge a partnership with them. Another of our aims was to invest in the creation of subsidiary companies; it was important that R1 had a presence close to major existing rubber purchasing and production centers. Eventually, we formed companies in Malaysia, Thailand, Japan, Vietnam, and—of course—Singapore. Over the years, we've expanded to a total of twelve locations in nine countries.

I believe an organization must exist for a purpose. Without a role to perform and a contribution to make, even the strongest companies become irrelevant and fade away. Purpose brings sustainability. To unite everyone in an organization toward a common goal, such as R1's ambition to be the world's number one rubber trader, the vision must be clear and inspiring to all.

Our *vision statement*, which encapsulates the company's overarching aspiration, expresses our desire "to be the number one global trading company in our field, redefining the industry with responsive solutions and contributing to the greater success of our partners in business." Our *mission statement*, by contrast, refers to the specific steps we take to make our vision a reality. At R1, our mission statement can be summarized in three words: serve, grow, prosper. This is also my personal mission statement. I believe that we should all be focused on creating something good in our lives while simultaneously contributing to the world around us.

At the foundation of a company, it's essential to develop a healthy and inspiring corporate culture based on shared goals, values, and beliefs. Among the group, there must be a strong sense of belonging and teamwork, augmented by an atmosphere of open communication where employees feel empowered to learn and share. When founding R1, I also wished to emphasize the importance of having fun at work. This combination of credibility, integrity, and the ability to have fun have driven our success in the decade and a half since R1 was founded. Our corporate culture is like a secret glue that binds together all the components of a healthy business.

It's not as easy as it sounds to build a business with such a strong corporate culture, yet culture is one of the most important elements of an organization. It's intangible and can appear invisible, especially to outsiders, yet it permeates every aspect of the company. I want everyone who works at R1 to feel that their contribution has meaning.

To succeed in this objective, we must find ways to serve *all* of our stakeholders, including suppliers, consumers, shareholders, employees, and industry partners. When we describe growth in our mission statement, we're not talking only about market size, innovation level, and range of product. We're also talking about a growth in service. Covering all of these bases allows us to earn the financial rewards, industry recognition, and stakeholder accolades we all desire.

This is why the intention to serve, grow, and prosper has become a trademark for us. It's on our business cards and it's featured in all of our publications. It's something we refer to as a guide along the path of success.

OWNING THE VISION AND MISSION

Valuable though a vision statement is, it's important that it's not merely an expression of the ideas of upper management. I've always wanted key team members and every employee to engage with the statement themselves, playing a part in discovering the company's purpose. I wanted them to *own* the company's mission and vision.

In the first few months of the company's existence, we organized a group retreat session with Arthur Anderson, with the intention of learning from the perspective of an outside consultant. By the end of the retreat, everyone who participated had played a role in coming up with ideas that became part of the vision statement. Even today, I'm always keen to ensure that people working with R1 feel a sense of ownership of the company's vision so that they believe in their work.

I've always hoped that people working with R1 feel a sense of purpose. I never wanted employees to come to work, obey managers like robots, then clock off and totally disengage. When I ask them who they work for, I don't want them to say R1; after all, what motivation would that provide? I want them to believe in the company vision and mission statement. They must feel that they are working for *themselves*, through the vehicle of R1. When they invest in themselves, they simultaneously invest in the company. With this mentality, they can feel a greater sense of purpose, and therefore a greater passion for what they produce.

People who work at R1 should feel that they are growing in experience and knowledge, and thereby increasing their own value. The company helps by investing in them. Even if they move on to another company, they should still feel that they leave R1 having found more insight, more self-esteem, and more meaning in their work. Why? Because they have contributed to the vision of our company. Their role is vital.

This is more than lip service. When I conduct exit interviews, I make a point of asking former employees how they feel about their time with R1. Most tell me that they have learned a great deal in a short space of time and that they appreciate the opportunities working with R1 has given them. To my mind, this illustrates that the company is genuinely dedicated to the learning and growth of employees, that our employees recognize the investment we make in them, and that they're happy to share their knowledge with others. I'm proud that this is part of R1's culture.

In this way, R1 is quite different from most other organizations. We want our people to understand their contribution toward the overall vision and mission of the company. Our people own their involvement because they become joint partners in the overall project. As a leader, I've always felt it essential to make employees feel that they play a key role in bringing the company's vision to life. This empowers them to take responsibility and to engage continuously with the goals of the group, almost like missionaries.

This is especially challenging in a remote work environment. We've developed R1 as a family residing in twelve different locations. Although employees are physically distant from one another, the culture, systems, and processes are all online, and everyone—no matter their location—is connected. This creates a feeling that we are one company and one family.

R1 employs people of eleven different nationalities, so it's not easy for them to come together seamlessly. There are natural cultural differences in communication style, habits, environment, and language. Yet we strive to find commonalities. One of the biggest challenges is convincing people to relax and enjoy their work. Singapore, as R1's main office, has always been the center of the company, and therefore the center of our group culture. Singaporean employees are used to an efficient rule-based atmosphere with a strong focus on productivity;

even coworkers who sit by one another rarely communicate on topics unrelated to work. The mood is highly impersonal, which can be stressful.

I come from a different environment and I've always been motivated to develop a group culture that is both hardworking and fun-loving. In Singapore, this has been a major challenge. In the early years of the company, I struggled for months to figure out how to shake up this atmosphere, a struggle compounded by the attitudes of several of my most knowledgeable and efficient senior Singaporean colleagues. While excellent at their jobs, they were quite rigid in temperament and behavior, which ran counter to my intentions.

I regularly gathered them together to discuss how the working environment could become lighter, explaining that every time I walked into the office I felt as though I were walking into a mortuary. It was common for me to find them working quietly at their computers, rarely interacting. It was a group culture completely different from the one I wanted to develop.

Initially, I sought to encourage them to move around and interact more. I organized occasions to meet for drinks outside the office, but even then, they rarely left their seats or mingled with other employees. I also brought in others, who wished to see the group become livelier, but the existing employees were so rigid that they refused to change.

Only when one of the most taciturn senior employees left R1 did the atmosphere begin to lighten. I installed music in the office and we went out together as a group more often. When mentoring employees or discussing important subjects with colleagues, I made a point of taking them to a local café instead of the office, to create a more conducive atmosphere for open sharing.

Nonetheless, it took a while for the Singaporean employees to open up and relax. Even today, the Singapore office of R1 is very different from some other locations, where employees lunch together and share common activities. After exhausting my capacity to create change, I realized that I needed to compromise. The relative austerity of my Singaporean colleagues has become a feature of R1, even a running joke to be shared when representatives of all our locations meet together.

AN EARLY CRISIS AVERTED

As you would expect, the process of growing an international company hasn't always been straightforward. Three and a half years after the formation of R1, the chief operating officer (COO), who had joined the company from Cargill, abruptly chose to leave, with the intention of joining a competitor and creating a new rubber trading company. Exacerbating the problem, key managers in R1's trading, operations, and finance departments, who had worked with him at Cargill, followed him out the door. This was a seismic event that could have wrecked our young company.

Worse than the initial business impact was the industry perception that R1 was floundering without key people who had joined from Cargill. I knew that if such a negative perception was allowed to spread unchecked, it would soon become reality. Competitors would pick off our best members of staff and we really *would* be floundering.

Fortunately, I was based close to the turmoil, in our Singapore office. I sensed the danger and understood the need to staunch the wound immediately so that we could right the R1 ship. Fortunately, one of Cargill's top managers from the United States had recently taken early retirement and moved to Malaysia to be with his partner. He was the man who had founded Cargill's rubber division and the mentor of our original COO—the one who had recently left.

I invited him to join R1 and, fortunately, he agreed. By replacing our original COO with someone clearly his superior, we instantly countered the belief that R1 was hemorrhaging talent. Existing R1 employees were reassured, the threat faded, and we once again set R1 on a path of productivity and success.

HAVING FUN TOWARD ONE MILLION

One of the best demonstrations of R1's commitment to creating a lighthearted atmosphere among employees is the daily "have fun toward one million" email sent to each member of staff. The idea—to mark each day of our journey toward an annual physical turnover of one million metric tons—came from one of my senior colleagues and has become so popular that employees notice, and raise an alert, if we miss a day.

Launched in December 2005, the project started as a way to boost employee motivation and bring people together. Jennifer Ho, my assistant in the Malaysia office, assigns everyone in our global offices a slot on an ongoing schedule. On any given day, the person who is assigned to contribute must share a joke, tell an amusing story, or share another fun contribution with the entire company, even if they are on leave or traveling.

Jennifer compiles these jokes and stories, which we hope will one day be published as a memento for employees and perhaps even sold in bookshops. The project has been so successful that, as we approached the goal in

2016, employees altered the subject line to "have fun toward *two* million." They didn't want it to stop.

GROWING A GLOBAL VIRTUAL COMPANY

R1's vision has become a rallying point for the company's large and diverse workforce, which I highlight at the opening of each annual staff group retreat. Sometimes I feel like a parrot, but the message is highly important. We even expect people going through a review to explain their understanding of the company's vision and mission statement. Sometimes we joke about the importance of these statements, for example by teasing employees that they will miss out on bonuses and increments if they can't repeat the company's vision when asked, but this too helps to keep everyone aligned and focused.

Structuring the company so that we work in various locations, connected online, plays a part in developing this culture. Everything is reported immediately and everyone in the company has access to relevant information. The transparency of online communication allows us to build a sense of collaboration even when we're hundreds or thousands of kilometers apart.

Nurturing empathy is a key element of this process. Most talented people have an ego, and it's easy to fall into the trap of thinking that we exist to provide answers and solutions to the problems of others. By practicing empathy, we remind ourselves to truly listen to others, not merely to react defensively. This is especially important when communicating online, without the cues that come from body language, tone of voice, and facial expression.

Teamwork has always been a huge part of our culture. Instead of naming a single leader, we opted instead to create leadership *teams* so that good ideas could be easily shared. Members of these teams can learn from the person next to them or connect with colleagues in different offices. Where necessary, they can challenge one another or work together to solve problems. We encourage them to be both candid and constructive; when everyone shares insights together, we generate ideas that no one could have come up with alone. The interests of the group always come first.

We're fortunate to work with extremely talented people, yet we take steps to ensure that no one is trying to out-compete the others in search of an ego boost. When a company contains a group of stars, some may try to shine brighter than the others. This desire to excel is positive, because we want to bring everyone on the team to their highest level so that the overall value of the team increases. However, we don't want individuals to jeopardize the success of the company in search of personal rewards. We emphasize that each person is good individually, but together we can all be better. We improve by sharing each other's experiences and looking at situations objectively rather than personally. As a small group operating in a challenging environment, we have little time or space for office politics.

There will always be challenges, constraints, and hurdles, but leaders strive to bring everyone together. At R1, our leaders are like athletic team managers or symphony conductors. We have enormous raw talent at our disposal; our best "strikers," "defenders," and "goalkeepers;" our finest "musicians." How do we bring them together to create harmony and achieve the desired results for the group?

Our leaders know they can't do this alone. A single leader may have a lot of experience and good ideas, but the people who execute the ideas achieve the results. They must be passionate about the vision and mission of the company. Their sense of ownership drives them to take responsibility; their sense of responsibility fuels a commitment to achieve results; their commitment inspires passion to serve, grow, and prosper. As we'll see in the next chapter, when all of these factors are in alignment, a company can experience outstanding growth.

CHAPTER FOUR

Growing the Company

With the sharp growth of the global automobile industry, the rubber industry has evolved hugely during the past several decades. For many years, rubber was highly sought after by European and American consumers, who appreciated its multiple applications. Grown predominantly in southern Asia, rubber traveled an enormous distance between growers and consumers. Due to this distance and the disconnection between growers and users, trading companies stepped in to facilitate transactions, sourcing rubber from where it was grown and distributing it to places where it was deficient.

In a less globalized world, the role of these companies was vital. They forged a link between growers and consumers that wouldn't otherwise have existed, becoming valued intermediaries. Their role required them to take ownership of the commodity, assuming considerable risk. They aimed to buy at low prices and sell the rubber they had purchased at an attractive profit. The commercial skills of these early traders were undeniable, although they also benefited from the prevailing lack of transparency in the industry during those early days.

It can be hard for us to remember a world without the internet, but these traders operated without easy access even to the telephone. They had only the telex and the telegraph, equipment that most young traders today have never heard of, let alone used.

For many years, the pure rubber trading industry was highly lucrative. Early traders made their fortunes in rubber, then invested in real estate, banking, and various other industries, where they built vast empires. Pure rubber trading, however, was already running into difficulties by the 1970s, when I entered the industry. It was still relevant, but the spread of information was starting to threaten the status of rubber traders as intermediaries. The number of players was growing and there was pressure for traders to adapt their activities and expand into other areas of the industry. Rubber-producing countries wanted to attract investors from the Western world so that various rubber items could be manufactured close to plantations, then sold in their higher-value finished form. These developments coincided with rapid developments in communication and technology, which eroded the advantages held by rubber traders.

Pure traders relied on privileged access to market information. When they began to lose that advantage, their business model began to falter. On the other hand, consumers, producers, and suppliers enjoyed more transparency, which brought improved market efficiency. Over time, profit margins for pure traders grew thinner and thinner; in the twenty-first century, rubber trading margins are like the space between a wall and a sheet of wallpaper—almost nonexistent.

In this highly competitive environment, innovative companies have attempted to adapt and remain relevant. One way in which they have tried to do this is by venturing into more non-trading, value-added services in addition to their pure trading function. For example, numerous companies have started warehousing their own product, financing it, and arranging the insurance, risk management, and shipment. They assume the role of a just-in-time, outsourced service provider.

Since the turn of the millennium, industry trends have further jeopardized the business of rubber trading. Producers and consumers have begun to communicate directly, believing that both will get better deals if they cut out the middleman. The flow of information from tree to end product has become increasingly transparent, with new technologies allowing farmers to know the prices their products sell for in different parts of the world.

Simultaneously, a new breed of traders has entered the market. These are nonphysical financial traders who use rubber as a financial derivative. They don't engage in the physical business of rubber trading; instead, they buy and sell contracts and futures options. Their presence has increased volatility and price distortions, squeezing margins even tighter. At times, physical rubber prices fail to reflect the true value of the commodity, because they don't include the actual costs of production, storage, and shipment. The changing market environment has turned today's rubber market into an entirely new one.

THE MARKET INNOVATION OF R1

When we founded R1, we recognized this changing environment. Our goal was to find a new way of doing business so that we could redefine the industry. At the time, most rubber trading companies were family owned. Very few corporations took part in rubber trading. Although these families drove the industry, we felt that there was an opportunity for us to compete as a global entity, which we did by merging the activities of MARDEC and Cargill Rubber Trading—the first a producer, the second a global trader. By combining the capabilities of both companies, we immediately became a global company with a presence in all major producing countries and consuming countries.

Redefine Industry Dynamics
The proposed joint venture provides a unique solution to this market.

This joint venture will transform the industry by providing a new mechanism, agile and strategically positioned to deliver large quantities of specialty rubber to downstream customers.

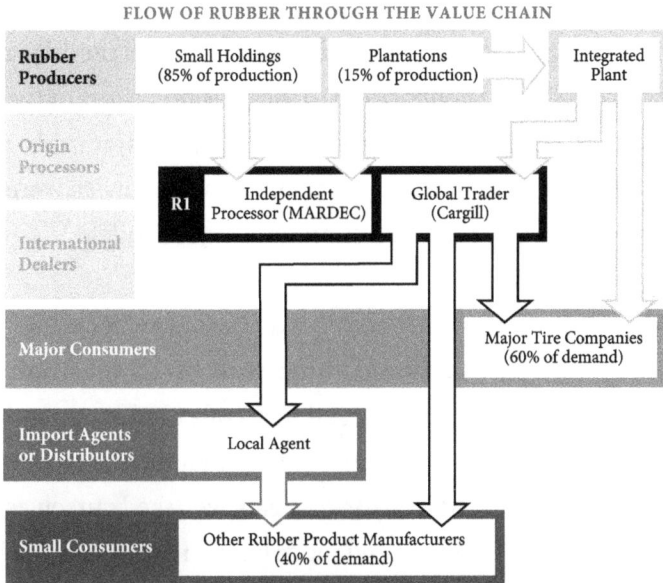

FLOW OF RUBBER THROUGH THE VALUE CHAIN

Rubber Producers	Small Holdings (85% of production)	Plantations (15% of production)	Integrated Plant

Origin Processors	R1	Independent Processor (MARDEC)	Global Trader (Cargill)	

International Dealers

Major Consumers		Major Tire Companies (60% of demand)

Import Agents or Distributors	Local Agent

Small Consumers	Other Rubber Product Manufacturers (40% of demand)

As a professionally run institution, we took pains to distinguish ourselves from the family-run businesses. Specifically, we wanted to develop solutions for both consumers and suppliers that enabled them to succeed in business. For an industry that had become stagnant, this approach was little short of revolutionary.

When we started R1, the rubber industry consisted of a few hundred players. On the consumer side, the biggest buyers were multinational tire companies such as Michelin, Goodyear, and Bridgestone. These tire companies had dealt with owner-operated traders for decades and the chance to work with a large, integrated corporation represented a fresh opportunity for them. We offered them a whole range of products from various origins, combined with a strong presence in both consuming and producing countries. We aspired to work with them in a partnership that contributed to the overall success of the industry. Since we were present in all the major rubber production countries, suppliers in those countries were immediately attracted to our new, unique model.

At this time, the commodity business was becoming extremely transactional. Buyers were increasingly focused on price, pushing sellers to offer half-cent and even quarter-cent discounts. For R1, joining this race to the bottom made little sense. Instead, we asked ourselves how we could stand out and move beyond a transactional focus. To do this, we identified needs that were going unmet and determined how we could fulfill them.

Here's an example: For both producers and consumers, maintaining the stability of their supply is an important consideration. When consumers deal with smaller sellers, they may purchase rubber at a specific price, then see the market price rise dramatically. In these circumstances, producers may default on a contract and seek higher prices elsewhere. This has happened, notably in 2008, when significant jumps in rubber prices exposed consumers to large losses. For rubber purchasers, this is a dilemma. They want to continue buying rubber, but they want to know that they will not be exposed to defaults or other financial damages.

At R1, we can promise them that, no matter how high—or low—the price of rubber, we will always honor contracts. For consumers, this is a huge advantage. We can sell far forward—as much as one or two years in the future—at fixed prices. Many choose to work with us even when our prices are slightly higher than those of our competitors, because our contracts are rock solid, and they know that they can rely on our integrity.

Also, we emphasized our business-partnership model to differentiate ourselves from the owner-operated, transaction-based model. We knew that we needed to operate from a new mindset, thinking of both buyers and sellers as our partners in business. We invested time, effort, and money to align everyone at R1 with this mindset because we knew that our partnerships would only succeed if we could build trust with our counterparts.

Establishing trust takes time. It requires a commitment

to prioritizing the relationship, not simply taking out as much profit as possible at the expense of a long-term partnership. To ensure that everyone at R1 understood the importance of this approach, we invested in training that inculcated a partnership mindset in everyone who worked at the company. No one else in the industry came close to matching this approach, and it set us apart from—and ahead of—our competitors.

THE STRUCTURE OF R1

Our early shareholders, MARDEC and Cargill, were huge companies, but they were ill-equipped to prosper in rubber trading because they lacked the flexibility and agility that smaller firms could offer. They were like oil tankers: large and powerful, yet unwieldy. We needed to find a way of combining the benefits of their size with the leanness and agility of a much lighter vessel—a speedboat.

The fundamental business proposition of R1 is our capacity to be partner-centric and enable business. This is embedded in the very DNA of our corporate culture.

R1's Business-Partner-Centric Model
A Key Tool to Grow Our Business,
a Strategic Differentiator in Saturated Markets

Customer service is becoming a key driver of value generation and strategic differentiation in an overcrowded marketplace.

FIVE KEY DRIVERS:

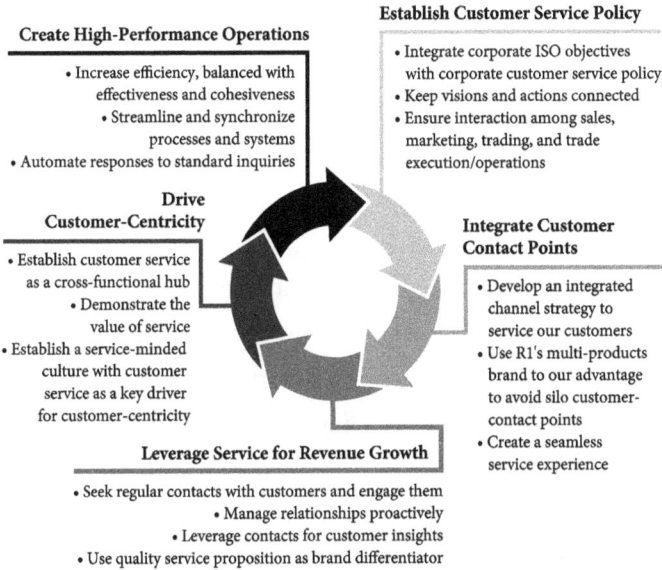

Create High-Performance Operations

- Increase efficiency, balanced with effectiveness and cohesiveness
- Streamline and synchronize processes and systems
- Automate responses to standard inquiries

Establish Customer Service Policy

- Integrate corporate ISO objectives with corporate customer service policy
- Keep visions and actions connected
- Ensure interaction among sales, marketing, trading, and trade execution/operations

Drive Customer-Centricity

- Establish customer service as a cross-functional hub
- Demonstrate the value of service
- Establish a service-minded culture with customer service as a key driver for customer-centricity

Integrate Customer Contact Points

- Develop an integrated channel strategy to service our customers
- Use R1's multi-products brand to our advantage to avoid silo customer-contact points
- Create a seamless service experience

Leverage Service for Revenue Growth

- Seek regular contacts with customers and engage them
- Manage relationships proactively
- Leverage contacts for customer insights
- Use quality service proposition as brand differentiator

To maximize our effectiveness, we established a core team in the head office, with small teams at all major producing and consuming locations. Each location, large and small, formed part of one virtual vehicle. We set up a sector trading system to meet the different needs of customers with diversified portfolios. Each sector represented rubber from a particular producing country. In trading terms, the purpose of each sector was to manage risk in a specific market or geographical area. We had six sectors covering all rubber origins and grades.

Sector one was the standard Indonesian rubber (SIR) sector. As the name suggests, it covered all standard Indonesian rubber origins. The second sector, standard Malaysian rubber (SMR) did the same for Malaysia. The Thai standard rubber (TSR) sector was based in Thailand, while the fourth sector encompassed standard Vietnamese rubber (SVR), and the fifth handled liquid latex. The last sector was for raw materials, which could be turned into finished products.

Each sector operated as a distinct business unit. This system dispersed responsibility for trading management to a range of different locations, and each sector had its own authority, limits, and profit and loss (P&L) responsibility. Empowering each sector to make decisions helped the company attract the best possible talents, while company-wide limits prevented us from overexposing ourselves to risk.

To redefine the industry, we had to be both agile and dynamic. Equally, it was important for the development of our business culture and for the growth of our teams that we offered people responsibility and the chance to take ownership of their working lives. This freedom was balanced by transparent reporting practices. Each sector reported both to the management sector and online, so representatives of every sector knew how much the others were handling and the prices at which they were selling.

In addition to the six sectors described above, we also created four specialized distribution sectors. Located predominantly in consumer regions such as China, India, the United States, and Eastern Europe, their role was in the distribution business. At the head office level, we established a management sector to oversee the activities of the other sectors. Naturally, this was where the more experienced trading managers worked.

In a trading company like R1, there are four key divisions: trading, operations, administration, and finance. The commercial activities of all the sectors and distribution areas come together with the risk management, finance and accounting, and operations departments, while the risk enterprise department oversees governance and compliance.

We felt it was essential that we spread responsibility throughout the company. Other companies operate under the auspices of a "super trader." In this scenario, the owner makes all the decisions, and everything is dependent on one person. We wanted to avoid this situation, so we created a team of trading heads. Despite basing themselves in different countries, they came together to work as a single virtual group. This system was important to keep the whole company strong, instead of allowing one powerful person to dictate to others.

The super trader represents a huge risk for trading companies, even among the large multinational corporations. If unsuccessful, they can seriously damage the company. If successful, they can leverage their influence to demand disproportionate rewards or leave and take team members with them, placing the company at risk.

Employing a super trader would have gone directly against our determination to develop a culture of learning and sharing. As the business underwent changes, we wanted a business environment rich in global experience, one that promoted healthy growth so people in all regions could learn from others.

Another key was maximum visibility. We wanted completed work to appear online immediately so that everyone in the company could benefit from the information. With twelve different locations and the best rubber trading talent in the world, I wanted as much assurance as possible that the company would thrive even if experienced people left.

To make these habits stick, we focused on developing a strong team and routinely brought in outside consultants to discuss team behavior and psychology. We knew that it was important for each employee to feel like an entrepreneur, with responsibility for their part of the business. With greater authority came more control and power, so they were motivated to do their best. For the same reason—wanting to maximize performance—we made a decision to reward employees generously.

THE IMPORTANCE OF RISK MANAGEMENT

The other side of our commitment to giving R1 employees autonomy has always been the necessity of risk management. As a rubber trading company, we are in the business of risk, so it's especially vital that we limit our exposure.

Consider the analogy of a ship in a rough sea. Without a steering wheel and rudder—systems of management and control—there's a high chance that the ship will drift aimlessly, fall into a precarious situation, and sink. How do we maintain control of the ship? We operate defined position limits, which prevent individuals from exposing the company to excessive risk.

Each sector is assigned a position limit which cannot be exceeded, except in consultation with the risk manager and the chief trading officer. Each temporary exception must be justified. Within these limits, however, each sector is fully empowered to use all the trading strategies at their disposal, including physical trading of rubber itself against futures trading, back-to-back physical trading, and futures-to-futures trading, along with spreads and directional trading.

Immediately on execution, all transactions in each sector are accurately reported. Whenever a trader makes a sale or a purchase, they must report it online to the entire group. This system serves several purposes: it delivers market transaction information to all global team members, while simultaneously establishing a built-in check. When everyone can see information online, errors come to light very quickly.

In addition to online reporting, traders must also generate position reports for the risk management, finance, and operations teams. These teams enforce strict compliance about position limits and value at risk (VaR). Any noncompliance is addressed by the enterprise risk manager.

In addition to these measures, we operate both a soft loss limit and a hard loss limit. When a trader reaches the soft loss limit, they are reminded to review their existing position and determine whether their actions will prove profitable in the long term. If they are confident about their position, they can still maintain it. When they reach the hard loss limit, however, they must immediately liquidate their position. These limits prevent them from exposing the group to any danger.

When I thought through how I wanted R1 to operate, I knew that it was imperative to avoid the temptation of relying on star traders. Instead, my goal was to create an efficient system that fostered continuous improvement, to sustain the company long term.

Workflow Process and Control Functions

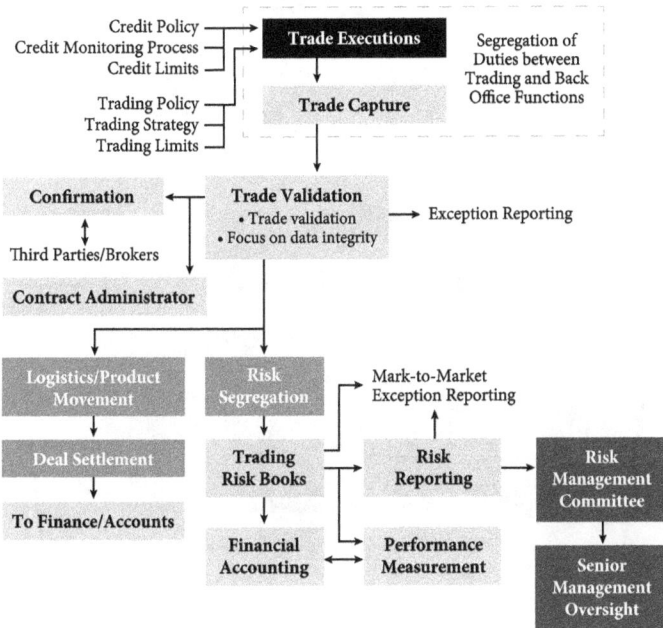

R1'S BLACK BOX

To maximize the potential for insight and growth, I created the R1 black box. In the marketplace, our performance and growth were always under a microscope, and representatives of other companies sometimes joked that we had a secret black box with a genie telling us what to do. We really *do* have a black box, but instead of a genie, it contains three compartments that have played an essential role in driving our success.

R1 GTS Black Box

| Market Analytics | GTS Sectors | GTS Mega |

MARKET ANALYTICS

The first compartment of the black box is market analytics. Our global traders need an understanding of the factors that impact rubber prices and their current trends. These factors are numerous, from the state of the world economy to the fundamentals of rubber demand and supply, from currency movements to global politics, technical indicators, and even weather patterns.

The trading-sector-heads team meets every Monday via conference call to discuss technical, macro, and fundamental factors and to share and exchange information. This meeting also represents an opportunity to challenge each other and update their viewpoints so that they can consistently make new and better decisions based on the available data. When we started R1, we knew that it was important to understand the industry landscape and take note of all the elements that could influence rubber prices.

Throughout R1, we've made sure to employ talented people in each major producing and consuming country, and to invest thoroughly in this network. Leveraging this network allows us to access vital information. Each team member, in their respective areas, analyzes relevant information. During the weekly global conference call, they share what they have learned during the previous week, then set their sights on the week ahead. These calls—and this system—reflect the strength of R1's network.

GTS SECTORS

The second compartment is known as GTS sectors. GTS stands for Global Trading System. Having established six sectors of operation and four areas of distribution, we assigned each sector to a sector head, assisted by their traders. The objective of each sector head is to become an expert in their local market so they can leverage that knowledge for the benefit of the company. Each sector head participates in a GTS sector conference call once per week, during which they submit a trading plan based on their projected activities over the following seven days.

These game plans describe what sector heads intend to buy and sell, the price ranges they anticipate, their trading strategies with the futures market, establish cut-loss limits, and their profit-potential projections. At the end of each call, the GTS sector coordinator summarizes strategies and targets for the entire group. This meeting—known as a game plan meeting—forms the basis of the sector heads' work. GTS sectors is the group's core revenue-generating area.

GTS MEGA

Our third compartment is GTS Mega, composed of key senior traders with a great deal of experience. In a commodity market such as rubber, opportunities to take big—or mega—positions occasionally arise. On average, this may happen two or three times per year. These mega positions represent both a high level of risk and a high level of reward. From the foundation of R1, we recognized that to make the most of these opportunities, we needed to meet regularly and proactively seek them. This was the genesis of GTS Mega.

When our senior traders see a big market opportunity, such as a directional advantage with a price increase or decrease, they alert the mega team. Their responsibility is to explain the parameters of the opportunity, citing the expected entry and exit levels, along with the potential for profit. In these scenarios, our traders also explain the potential loss and determine the level at which we will liquidate our position if their predictions prove inaccurate. Plans are discussed by key experienced traders, who evaluate their potential; if all agree with a high degree of conviction, the group takes the mega position.

Mega opportunities don't represent guaranteed success. Unlike owner-operators, who can take a position and exit quickly if the situation goes downhill, corporations must build a system to predict risk in advance, exercise strict discipline, and comply with risk management strategies.

ESSENTIAL TRADING TECHNIQUES

At times, it may be unclear how pure traders make money. As I define it, the key principle is to seek out inefficiency in the marketplace. Traditionally, traders earned income by simultaneously buying from one source and selling to another. In the modern marketplace, however, such opportunities are extremely rare. Groups such as R1 must seek out other ways to make money in the marketplace, which we'll discuss below.

Directional trading is a strategy based on our assessment of the direction of rubber prices. We take two basic positions. If we believe, based on a thorough analysis of the market, that rubber prices in a specific market will rise, we take a *long* position. This means that we buy in the expectation that, when prices rise to an appropriate level, we will be able to sell or liquidate our position and make a profit. If we believe that prices are liable to fall, we adopt a *short* position. In other words, we sell in the expectation that we will be able to buy more cheaply at a later date.

Within the rubber industry, directional trading takes place in various types of markets. The first is the physical or cash market, in which traders accept delivery of the underlying commodity (when taking a long position) or undertake to provide the product to consumers (when taking a short position). The second is the futures market, in which no physical product changes hands. In this scenario, the underlying position is usually closed prior to the expiry of the underlying contract.

Directional trading can be lucrative. On the other hand, if we make a mistake and take an erroneous position, it can be very costly, so it's essential that we always make a careful analysis before making a decision.

R1 is essentially a spread trader. Unlike a directional strategy, in which either a long position or a short position is adopted independently, a spread trade involves executing both a long position and a short position simultaneously. The objective is to earn money based on the projected *change* in the relationship between the long position and the short position. Let's look at an example.

Imagine that the current price differential between two different types of rubber on the Singapore market, SICOM 3 and SICOM 20, is US $135 per ton. We anticipate that SICOM 3 will strengthen relative to SICOM 20, so we simultaneously buy SICOM 3 and sell SICOM 20. Now suppose that our prediction proves correct and the price differential between SICOM 3 and SICOM 20 widens to $375 per ton. We can then sell SICOM 3 and buy SICOM 20 at a profit of $240 per ton.

The underlying impetus of spread trading is a bet that one commodity will move more favorably than another. From a risk management perspective, it is less risky than a single directional trade. Like any trade, however, it is not without risk. There is a possibility that both commodities will move in the opposite direction to the one we expect. If this happens, we will lose money. Additionally, the lower risk means that spread trading tends to yield lower returns than directional trading.

Like directional trading, spread trading can take place in either the physical market or the futures market. In both situations, the purpose of the trade remains the same; to profit from the changing price relationship between two commodities. Let's look at some opportunities for traders in futures spread trading.

Inter-Commodity Spread Trading

As described above, this involves purchasing one commodity and selling another at the same time. This strategy is usually executed within a single market, for example, SICOM.

Calendar or Time Spread Trading

This involves buying and selling the same commodity across different calendar months at the same time. For example, we might purchase SICOM 3 for delivery in July and sell in August. If a trader buys for delivery in a near month and sale in a deferred month, this time spread strategy is known as a bull spread. A trader making this bet will earn money if the July price strengthens more than the August price. In the reverse case—a trader who sells July and buys August—the strategy is known as a bear spread. Naturally, the opposite is true here; a trader making this bet will make money if the commodity price weakens in July more than it does in August. Again, this strategy is executed within the same futures market.

Geographical Spread Trading

There is more than one rubber futures market, so traders can also bet on the relationships between them. For example, we may choose to buy in the Tokyo (TOCOM) futures market and trade in the Singapore market (SICOM). A trader may sell Nov TOCOM and buy SICOM 20 while the price differential between the two is $395 per ton. When that price differential narrows to $195 per ton, the trader will earn $200 per ton.

BASIS TRADING

Strictly speaking, basis trading is a form of spread trading. It is a financial strategy founded on purchasing a specific commodity and selling a related derivative. Basis trading is driven by the desire to minimize risk: A trader may take long and short positions in two different securities in order to profit from the convergence of their values. Meanwhile, he may sell a futures contract to manage the risk he incurs from his physical contract.

The futures market generally falls in tandem with the physical market. In the event that prices decline, the trader's loss from his long position on the physical trade will be somewhat mitigated by the gains he makes from his short position on the futures market.

THE VALUE OF DISCIPLINE

At R1, we engage actively in all the forms of trading and risk management described above. Each strategy is executed only after conducting a thorough risk management assessment, including analysis of various fundamental, technical, and economic factors, both microeconomic and macroeconomic. We only execute strategies when we believe the risk-reward ratio is in our favor.

To further minimize our risks, we operate a cut-loss mechanism, whereby we close existing trades if outcomes fall significantly outside our expectations. This reduces the risk that individual traders will stick stubbornly to loss-making strategies.

Although there's nothing secret or proprietary about rubber trading, we are different from other types of traders. We organize ourselves differently, with unique systems, processes, and controls.

Arguably, our key differentiating factor is discipline. Owner-operator setups make trading decisions based on the beliefs of one person or, at most, a small team.

Owners can make a lot of money, but they can also take big losses, perhaps so big that they're forced to close.

As a group, one of our non-negotiable principles is to ensure full compliance with risk management at all times. Other trading companies may not have this type of management. When we formed R1, we realized that a successful pure rubber trading company needed to be lean and mean. We had to be focused, and we needed talented, experienced people—people who were motivated, with an entrepreneurial mindset.

As we'll discuss in the next chapter, trading rubber is a risky business. It requires strong systems and, above all, world-class risk management. We know that to get ahead we must expose ourselves to risk. Yet we also understand how important it is to mitigate risk if we are to consistently succeed.

CHAPTER FIVE

Enterprise Risk Management

Rubber trading is one of the most volatile trading commodities in the world. It's a high-risk industry with no guarantee of success. The industry consists of two intertwined markets: the physical market, where buyers and sellers trade physical rubber in different forms and from different origins, and the futures market, comprising forward futures and options contracts. Participants in the futures market include both physical and nonphysical traders. The nonphysical traders are primarily investors and commodity fund speculators.

While our primary business is based in the former, we must also engage in the latter to manage our risk. The presence of both physical and nonphysical players brings price volatility and liquidity to the market. We embrace this volatility—as a source of potential profit—rather than avoid it, and we seek to operate a system that allows us to maximize profit while minimizing loss. We call this "enterprise risk management."

Enterprise risk management (ERM) is a comprehensive, fully integrated risk management system that identifies potential risks, assesses them, and addresses their potential to cause damage. All of our trading decisions are taken with reference to this process. It's a flowing, ongoing system that permeates the entire company, our people, and all of our activities at every one of our twelve locations. It also assures our shareholders and board of directors that we have the ability to align everything we do to make our business a success, although we are in a risky business with volatile price movements.

As both a global trading company and a virtual company, R1 is a highly complex entity. Trading happens around the world, at all hours, and is affected by events ranging from the political climate and financial markets to international and domestic conflict.

Enterprise risk management is necessary to ensure that we set clear parameters determining how much risk we will take and that we don't exceed those limits. With this system in place, our traders, who function as entrepreneurs within the auspices of the company, have the confidence and courage to operate in this complex and volatile market. They're free to take ownership of their trading decisions and strategies. The key character trait of a good trader is discipline. When a trader makes a trading decision, they aim to secure a reward. Nonetheless, they know that if something goes wrong with the deal, they will lose out.

Good traders analyze trading decisions to determine the risk/reward ratio. If a trade has a risk/reward ratio of 100/30, traders know that they could make a hundred dollars, but they could also lose thirty. If they make the decision to make the trade, they know the risks.

Without strong risk management, companies in our line of work may be exposed to serious business losses. We understand that in a volatile sector such as rubber trading, there is always the possibility that we will take losses. We must be certain, however, that these losses are never so great that they prove fatal. Without ERM, we would be like sea captains navigating violent sea conditions in a ship without radar. It is essential for our survival. This approach has become part of our corporate culture, flowing through all aspects of the company's business and operations. It's part of R1's DNA, involving all team members and all company activities.

For a clearer picture of the key elements of R1's risk management practices, consider figure 5.1. We know that risk is part of our business. By accepting this fact, we put ourselves in a position to collect information about the risks we face, analyze their severity, and manage them to ensure that they don't cause the company major harm.

Risk Framework: Governance and Practices

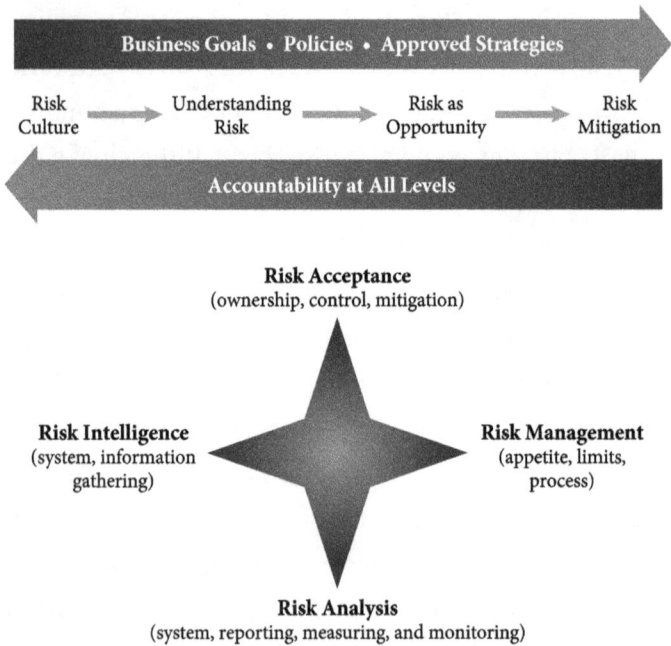

Business Goals • Policies • Approved Strategies

| Risk Culture | Understanding Risk | Risk as Opportunity | Risk Mitigation |

Accountability at All Levels

Risk Acceptance
(ownership, control, mitigation)

Risk Intelligence
(system, information gathering)

Risk Management
(appetite, limits, process)

Risk Analysis
(system, reporting, measuring, and monitoring)

THE ERM FRAMEWORK

R1's risk management framework is composed of three key areas:

RISK GOVERNANCE

Risk governance refers to our overall organizational structure and corporate culture, which promotes risk recognition while encouraging R1's traders to seize opportunities. It outlines the company policy and strategy, and clearly defines the boundaries of responsibility and authority.

With the involvement of the board of directors, corporate-level decision makers, and the trading teams from various business units, the risk governance network is fully integrated and feeds guidelines into the company from the top down. The board approves and defines specific risk parameters, which ultimately represent the risk of the entire company.

DAY-TO-DAY RISK MANAGEMENT

Risk governance is complemented by day-to-day risk management, which functions independently under the leadership of the head of enterprise risk management, who reports directly to the managing director and the board of directors.

RISK MANAGEMENT COMMITTEE

This top-down governance structure is also influenced by the risk management committee, which comprises board members and senior traders. The committee identifies our risk exposure, analyzes individual risks, and determines whether they are low, moderate, or serious. The finance team, the risk management team, and the traders work together to complete this analysis.

This risk management framework incorporates all the key areas of R1's business, such as strategies, operations, and market and credit exposure. The whole system is further augmented by internal and external audits, while we use IT to capture all positions online, with key metrics reported instantly to relevant people throughout the organization.

These three elements contribute to a strong risk management awareness culture. We strengthen this culture by educating employees about its necessity, by adopting common risk language, and by checking periodically to ensure that it is in proper working order.

Instilling an awareness of risk management into our many employees is essential to the success of R1. Many companies operate solid risk management systems but neglect the vital importance of creating awareness and instilling discipline among traders. To ensure that our risk management is as effective as possible, all of our traders complete in-house training programs on risk, taught by senior team members.

A complementary component involves regular checks on the effectiveness of risk management within the group. This is made possible by the online reporting of every trade that takes place under the auspices of R1. The risk management team also captures information so that its members understand what traders are doing and can assess risk levels.

Figure 5.2 illustrates the people—and the processes—responsible for managing R1's exposure to risk, from the board of directors to the risk management committee and the front-office traders. Each has a unique role to play in understanding, assessing, and addressing risk.

Control System

*Understanding of trading exposure
and its impact on global exposure is key.*

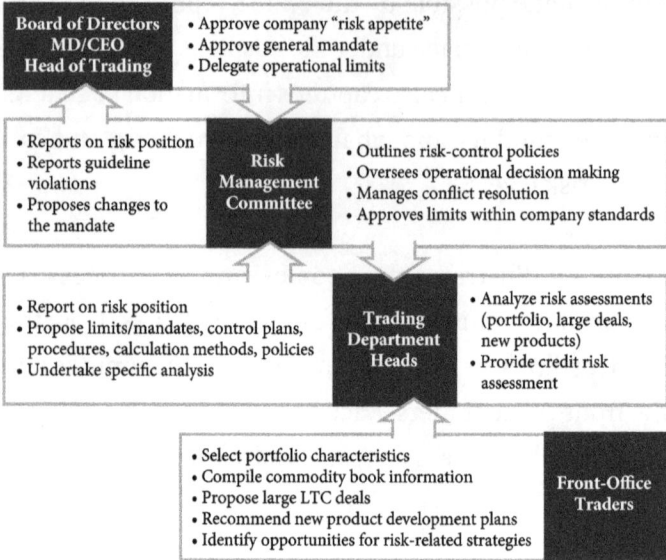

Board of Directors MD/CEO Head of Trading	• Approve company "risk appetite" • Approve general mandate • Delegate operational limits

• Reports on risk position • Reports guideline violations • Proposes changes to the mandate	**Risk Management Committee**	• Outlines risk-control policies • Oversees operational decision making • Manages conflict resolution • Approves limits within company standards

• Report on risk position • Propose limits/mandates, control plans, procedures, calculation methods, policies • Undertake specific analysis	**Trading Department Heads**	• Analyze risk assessments (portfolio, large deals, new products) • Provide credit risk assessment

• Select portfolio characteristics • Compile commodity book information • Propose large LTC deals • Recommend new product development plans • Identify opportunities for risk-related strategies	**Front-Office Traders**

FIVE CORE AREAS OF RISK

R1's enterprise risk management system covers five primary areas:

CORPORATE RISK GOVERNANCE

We operate in nine different countries and must ensure that we remain within the rules and legal boundaries of each of those countries. This is especially true in cases where we're a foreign entity. In some companies, foreign entities fall under greater scrutiny than domestic companies, making it especially important that we comply with all legal boundaries and industry regulations.

We make it a policy to monitor the activities and integrity of R1's management in every one of the countries in which we operate. We employ reputable legal, corporate, and financial advisors to assure the board that our corporate governance is watertight.

TRADING AND FINANCIAL RISK

Other areas of governance include trading risk and financial risk. The former is the biggest risk we face. If fluctuations in market prices were not mitigated, they could easily cause the company's downfall. To protect against this, we use various mitigation and risk tolerance tools to manage our commodity risk, liquidity risk, quality risk, and market and product diversification risk. Each of these areas must be assessed and managed effectively to ensure that we conduct business confidently and empower our global traders.

Financial risk relates to liquidity, interest rates, counterparty credit, and cash flow management. Regulating and controlling these areas of risk falls under the auspices of the trading, operations, and finance teams, managed by the chief financial officer.

OPERATIONAL RISK

The second core risk area is operational risk. This is a stable category, unaffected by market price movements. It includes concerns such as shipment issues, damaged cargoes, quality complaints, and documentation errors. Another potential risk in this area comes when traders fail to report trades or exceed permitted limits.

In addition, we must manage risk arising from our activities in partnership with other companies, such as suppliers and customers. This is known as counterparty risk. Should one of our customers default on a contract, for example, we could see an impact on our own financial status. For this reason, we operate a robust counterparty risk assessment system.

IT RISK

As a virtual company, our third area of core risk is IT. Were our online systems to suffer unnecessary or unplanned downtime, the consequences could be disastrous. As a diffuse company, we rely heavily on these systems. They form the backbone of the company and provide us with all the tools we need to manage and control risk. This is the IT risk associated with our business. Therefore, we employ both an in-house team and an external team who protect the company's IT systems from the risk of disruption.

Our final core risk is HR. We take every precaution to keep our employees happy. The company functions as a family and every team member at R1 is a valuable asset. Our HR policy is structured to provide each member of the company with all the necessary training and development they need to feel fulfilled at work. We understand that when team members achieve their goals, the company achieves its goals.

Nonetheless, there are also risks in this area. If we were to suddenly lose a raft of employees, it would have a considerable negative impact on the company's fortunes. This is why we take pains to put in place policies, structure, and oversight to ensure that we don't expose ourselves to the risks of high employee turnover.

Three years after we formed R1, an entire group of senior-level employees from one location all left the company suddenly. Due to their high rank, there was a risk that their departure could have a negative impact on the entire operation. They certainly believed that it would. When I first conceived of R1, I knew that the people would make the company. I hoped that, by operating with this principle in mind, we could limit the risk of an exodus, but I also understood that I couldn't be 100 percent certain that employees would be loyal.

After the above-mentioned employees left R1, news of our predicament reached the rest of the rubber trading market. Most people thought that we would suffer in the wake of such a large-scale departure. Thankfully, we managed to avert a catastrophe. We had installed a system that enabled our key leaders at each location to step in and run the operations of a different location if core team members left. The system worked perfectly, and the business ran as smoothly at all of our locations as it had when we had a full team.

The best way to avert danger is to expect it to happen, so I have always taken the attitude that it's essential to be prepared for negative scenarios. The human resources risk constitutes a very real threat. At any time, a team member could tell me that they're leaving the company. I never want people to leave, but I always anticipate the possibility.

This is another reason why R1 doesn't employ super traders. Instead, we have a system of trading heads, who rotate periodically, spread across various locations, from Singapore to Malaysia to Japan. If one leaves, we can easily mitigate the loss.

A subsidiary area of risk is business continuity. All our centers of operation are interconnected, so we cannot afford to see one of them cease operations. This type of hiccup would cause problems for all our counterparts. Recognizing this risk, we have established a simple system where, in the event of one location becoming nonoperational for any reason, another location can immediately take over and continue operations, without any substantial downtime.

This system was tested in 2002 when the entire world was affected by the deadly severe acute respiratory syndrome (SARS) epidemic. There was a threat that entire countries or regions of countries would shut down to control the disease. We feared that our business continuity would suffer, but fortunately it passed the test and reassured us that R1 would remain operational during a cataclysmic event.

Figure 5.3 shows how we determine which risks are most important. Managing minor risks is no use if we overlook risks that could lead to major catastrophes. Therefore, we must understand which risks—such as rubber price volatility—pose the greatest threat to R1's smooth operation, and which—such as reporting and process-based risks—are less crucial (albeit still important).

R1 Risk Matrix

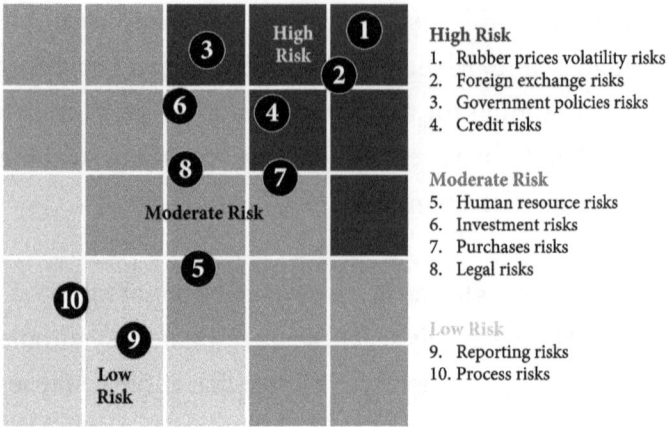

High Risk
1. Rubber prices volatility risks
2. Foreign exchange risks
3. Government policies risks
4. Credit risks

Moderate Risk
5. Human resource risks
6. Investment risks
7. Purchases risks
8. Legal risks

Low Risk
9. Reporting risks
10. Process risks

THE IMPORTANCE OF RISK MANAGEMENT SYSTEMS

Ever since R1's inception, Cargill has played a role in establishing the importance of enterprise risk management. When we established our system, Cargill sent people from the United States to assist us in following its philosophy.

As discussed in previous chapters, the majority of trading companies are relatively small, run by owner-operators. These companies are dominated by the personality of their owners. Therefore, they don't perceive a need for concrete risk management systems. In crises, responsibility for making decisions falls on the shoulders of the owner.

For a group as large as R1, however, this approach is

untenable. Aside from the potential damage the company could incur if we fail to mitigate risk, we also need to persuade external partners—such as banks—of our stability. When banks lend us money, they are exposed to plentiful risk. To reassure them, we provide them with a transparent review of our state of operations. This helps them to feel comfortable about working with us.

As an illustration, let's imagine that we have capital of $60 million. In this scenario, banks can lend us up to $500 million to finance trade. They will only do this, however, if they trust that we have a good risk management system in place, disciplined traders, and a good track record of performance. This setup fuels the company's growth. We can make good use of the financial support we receive from banks to grow the business, thereby strengthening that relationship once again.

Our counterparts, such as rubber suppliers and customers who purchase rubber from us, are also reassured by our risk management system. They know that we have strong risk management practices in place and support from the banks, so they feel confident in doing business with us.

Good risk management might seem strict, but it also creates freedom for our traders. Within predetermined limits, it empowers them to make decisions. It also allows our shareholders and board of directors to sleep soundly at night, knowing that the system we have in place to manage risk is robust. If they are ever concerned, they can take heart from the internal and external audits we conduct to ensure that our risk management systems are effective.

Over many years, strong risk management becomes a habit adopted by everyone in the company. Nonetheless, we must ensure that we continually enhance our risk management in the face of changing market conditions. To do this, we undertake an annual review of risk management functionality.

We also hire external consultants to analyze the system and propose enhancements. In the past, we've used consultants from all over the globe, including Switzerland, India, and the United States. Ultimately, risk management is an essential navigational tool, so it's vital that we review it both from the inside and the outside to keep improving.

The business environment doesn't stand still, and neither can we. The rapid pace of global technological change has a huge impact on global trading. The emergence of powerful computer processing capabilities and algorithms allows new players, such as speculators and commodity funds, to enter the industry. Developments such as these drive a lot of volatility within our environment, making it even more important that we sustain and improve our risk management framework.

Risk management must be more than a framework written on paper and left in a drawer. Policies must be clear, and good habits must be formed. To remain relevant and continue our growth, we need to find ways to get ahead of the curve. An effective and agile enterprise management system that constantly evolves is fundamentally important for keeping R1 relevant on a sustainable basis. Risk management is not static, and it's not a public relations tool. It must be practiced continuously, and it must lift up and drive everyone in the company to achieve the goals that underlie our corporate culture.

In the next chapter, we'll discuss the most important aspect of R1: the people.

CHAPTER SIX

A Global Family

As a pure rubber trading company, R1 doesn't possess any physical assets such as factories and machines. Our business is built on people. It is the people who work at R1 who make the company great. Throughout the industry, we're recognized for employing more talented trading heads than our competitors. In short: our people are the envy of the industry.

Our diverse team consists of people from eleven different countries. Many members of our key management team have accrued more than twenty-five years of experience in the industry, and I've always felt that their pedigree is essential to R1's success. Taken together, the global leadership team brings more than five hundred years of combined rubber trading experience to the organization. I myself have spent more than forty-three years of my life in the rubber industry. Additionally, more than 60 percent of the people on R1's leadership team have been with the company since its formative years, and our overall employee retention rate is exceptionally high.

When we formed R1, it was of paramount importance to me to work alongside great people. Equally important, I wanted to ensure that we retained those people, because I knew they were the key to sustainable success. As the founder of a company, it's natural to have ambition and passion to excel, but no leader can make a company great alone. We all need to surround ourselves with team members who are more capable than ourselves. In the end, success depends on the team members we choose. It's important that we all share the same aspirations, passion, energy, and dedication, and that each person embraces the company outlook as their own.

As I've already described, my goal when I founded R1 was to turn it into the number one global trading company in the world. To do this, I knew we had to contribute to the greater success of all our partners and create an effective corporate culture—one based on the company's strategic direction and expressing a unifying philosophy.

In the early stages, all key management members were intently involved in developing this unifying vision. They worked to identify our core competencies, assess our external environment, create our key strategies, and establish performance measures. They also helped me monitor the implementation of our strategies.

The three most powerful words that summarized our company's mission have always been "serve," "grow," and "prosper." These words have fostered a team spirit that has pushed us toward peak performance. Even today, we call ourselves the R-wonders. We're a cohesive virtual company spread across the world that operates as a single united entity—all for one, and one for all, just like the Three Musketeers.

We established a strategic management culture that clearly connected our vision and mission with our values, our desired strategic objectives, and our company and individual objectives. This culture formed the DNA of the company and set us apart as a unified global family. Nonetheless, the process wasn't always straightforward.

Prior to founding R1, I led a merger which brought an Italian manufacturer of latex thread to Malaysia. The logistical aspects of the merger were quite straightforward. Integrating people from Italy and Malaysia, who had differing cultural backgrounds, mannerisms, and food preferences, was a lot more complex!

When the time came to create R1, therefore, I was prepared for the difficulties inherent in bringing together diverse groups of people. Both MARDEC and Cargill offered valuable practices, processes, and systems. Similarly, both companies employed outstanding people who had a lot to contribute to R1. Integrating the process was quite simple. Integrating people with distinct competencies and outlooks was a significant challenge.

MARDEC was a processing company with a proven sales and marketing track record. Cargill was a reputable global trading company with strong risk management capabilities. We needed both sets of skills to build R1 into a successful global company. But how could we forge two separate workforces into a single organization?

While I understood that this would be a challenge, I underestimated how differently the two groups felt about their abilities and the abilities of their new colleagues. People from both MARDEC and Cargill believed in their own superiority.

Cargill's traders, coming from a multinational background, rated their skills highly and thought less of those whose background lay in processing. Meanwhile, traders from MARDEC found those from Cargill snobbish, especially considering that MARDEC was the largest shareholder in R1. MARDEC employees felt that MARDEC had played a role in keeping Cargill's traders in a job, so it was inappropriate for Cargill's traders to look down on them. While these two factions saw their differences as a problem, I felt that these same differences represented R1's greatest strength.

Even with this knowledge, however, I made an error of judgment. Coming from the MARDEC side of the partnership, I was particularly keen to ensure that those who had joined R1 from Cargill felt comfortable and welcome. I wished to make it clear that they were an essential part of the new team. Unfortunately, this led to some resentment among members of staff from MARDEC.

Perhaps you're familiar with the biblical parable of the prodigal son. A father has two sons, one of whom remains loyal to him throughout and one who departs, behaves badly, and eventually repents and returns to the family homestead. The father forgives his repentant son—the prodigal—so completely that the son who has loved and stood by his father all along becomes angry. Why, he wonders, is he not similarly appreciated?

This was my situation following the merger that led to the founding of R1. I made such an effort to welcome the new members of the team that my original team at MARDEC felt that their "father" was treating his new stepsons better than his loyal progeny. My move to Singapore, where Cargill's Asia Pacific division was based, exacerbated this perception.

While I realized there was no way to eliminate this gap immediately, I set about addressing it. Just as two people in a quarrel may be reconciled when they focus on a common enemy, I felt that the two factions of R1 could be united with a focus on a common goal. I engaged an external consultant, took all the employees to an off-site retreat, and engaged them in our search for a vision and mission.

Spending time together in a beautiful place, with a shared objective, started the process of melting the ice. People began to see themselves not as former employees of MARDEC and Cargill, but as part of a new team. Over time, with conscious effort, openness, and a vision and mission each one of them could commit to, they bonded into a global family. From that day forward, the experience shaped the way I approached the task of managing people.

NURTURING TEAMWORK

Why are religious people so passionate and energetic? It's because they are inspired by a concept they believe in. Bringing people together, centered on a mission, is a little like starting a religion.

Corporate culture is based on shared values. Of all these values, the most important is teamwork. People make a company great, but a conducive corporate culture turns even ordinary people into a great team.

There are several key values that form the foundation of teams. The first is clarity. To succeed, team members must feel clearly that they are working toward a common vision and that their organization exists for a purpose. Shared beliefs drive passion, while clear values unify teams.

The second pillar of teamwork is empowerment. In business, we need all of our key leaders to think and act like entrepreneurs. If one person can inspire the rest of his team to feel a sense of empowerment, they will be highly motivated to do great work. This is only possible when people understand their responsibilities and know that they have the power to make good decisions. Empowerment makes people committed, responsible, and accountable for their contributions to the team and to the overall company.

Open communication serves as the third pillar of teamwork. Team communication must be based on honesty, candor, and respect. To achieve success in a pressurized environment, team members must trust one another, just like any other family. Each person must understand the personalities of other members of their team and complement them accordingly.

Team members should be curious—the fourth pillar of teamwork. Being part of a group requires people to see things from different perspectives, so each person can learn from the others. This brings the entire team to another level. To perform well in the face of daunting challenges, it's vital for team members to nurture the ability to learn and grow together.

This leads to the fifth pillar of teamwork—maturity. Maturity is most visible when team members find ways to resolve conflicts together. The interests of the company must be placed above the interests of individuals, and operating from this perspective brings out a rich seam of maturity in team members. Conversely, it can also reveal the limitations of those who aren't committed to prioritizing teamwork above their individual goals.

The final pillar of a solid team is the ability to have fun. Team members should enjoy getting together outside the work environment, preferably in an informal and relaxed setting. At R1, we often go out for drinks together. In some countries, we visit karaoke bars, which present a great opportunity to relax and unwind together. In the company's early years, the global leadership team met for team-building sessions and offsite retreats, often at retreats by the sea or golf resorts, where the setting established feelings of openness and friendship.

I want everyone who works at R1—in all of our global locations—to be as passionate as I am about the company, so I focus a lot of time and energy on achieving a positive spirit and solid teamwork within the company. It's important to me that the company is cohesive and unified, and that individuals are empowered to give their best.

You may be wondering how the values described here operate in practice. In other companies, one or two people normally make all major decisions. At R1, the leaders of each location are involved in this process with input from their teams. For example, the trading team gets together via video conference on a weekly basis. They use this call to discuss upcoming business, along with the challenges and opportunities they're encountering in the marketplace. This is always a team discussion, with outcomes determined by the entire team, together.

As a virtual company, we are privy to a lot of information. It's important that we use this information to arrive at strategies and action plans collaboratively. When a team is aligned and focused on the group's objectives, it's easy to establish the best ways to take advantage of opportunities and to mitigate marketplace risks. Groups do best when they're honest with one another, when they're spontaneous, and when they engage in constructive dialogue. Above all else, the needs of the team must be paramount, so that ideas synergize into solutions.

We believe that more heads are better than one. We participate in weekly meetings, monthly meetings, and annual meetings with many different objectives, but one thing remains the same: we strive for cohesiveness so that we can arrive at the best outcome together.

A good corporate culture that fosters teamwork breeds high employee self-esteem. Employees understand the direction of the company and they know how their involvement contributes to the accomplishment of company goals. They recognize that their contribution has an impact, so they are motivated by a desire to make a positive difference.

When employees feel valued, they invest in learning about the company, their role, and how they can make a difference. This is reinforced by a culture of open communication and transparency. Every day, employees have the opportunity to increase their sense of self-worth and the value they deliver to the company.

This leads to a feeling of accomplishment and career satisfaction, a process that swiftly becomes self-reinforcing. Once the ball is rolling in a positive direction, personal maturity and stability naturally follow. Employees also leave work fulfilled, which supports a healthy and happy family life.

Over the years, I have found that being part of a global team elevates the outlook of the people who work at R1. When new people join the company, I sit down with them and—lightheartedly—ask them why they joined R1. Almost invariably, their initial answer is that they want to contribute to the firm's success. If this is the case, I feel sad for them. I share my philosophy that I want them to feel that they are working for themselves. Of course, they must earn their salary, but if they feel that they are working for themselves they will seek to maximize their learning. Why? Because they will see each day at work as an investment in themselves and their future.

When I welcome a new employee to R1, I explain that this philosophy also allows me to understand my exact contribution to the group. For people in the early stages of a career, that contribution may be quite small, but it still connects with the company's overall goals and aspirations. This realization is a big self-esteem boost. People who invest in themselves find it easy to grow and to go home fulfilled at the end of the day. They don't sit like robots at their desk all day. They understand that they are making a contribution to something greater than themselves. When they do this, their spirit and mood are lighter, an effect that ripples out to their colleagues and loved ones.

Most companies recognize that a good corporate culture will pave the way to success. In fact, I don't know of a single company that doesn't employ consultants for this reason. Yet it's one thing to understand this in principle. It's much more difficult to actually build a strong, authentic corporate culture.

Companies that fail in this objective usually do so because they don't have a solid foundation on which to build. Many neglect important qualities such as teamwork, team spirit, open communication, and growth and development. Many smaller, family-owned trading companies live in fear that their experienced employees, in whom they've invested heavily, will leave for greener pastures or start their own business. This fear isn't completely unfounded; I've seen it happen countless times, especially among the millennial generation.

By contrast, R1 is recognized and even envied for our work in this area. It's obvious to observers that our R-wonders feel a strong sense of belonging, that they are highly motivated, and that they're passionate about their contributions to the company. These experiences breed loyalty. Our team members feel a strong sense of loyalty both to the team and the company, a fact that is reflected in our retention rate.

Over the years, headhunters have persistently tried to lure away several of our key managers. They come on behalf of our competitors, both old and new, to make enticing offers at substantial preferential terms. Rarely do they succeed in convincing our top managers to depart for another company. Our retention rate, especially of our most senior employees, speaks volumes for the dedication, commitment, and loyalty of our employees. Our strength lies in our people, and our investment in them has given us a competitive edge.

This approach is illustrated by figure 6.1, which details our strategic management culture, and by figure 6.2, which outlines our corporate strategy map. Each part of the culture builds on other elements. When we work together to develop a strong culture, we are unbreakable.

R1 Strategic Management Culture (R1 SMC)

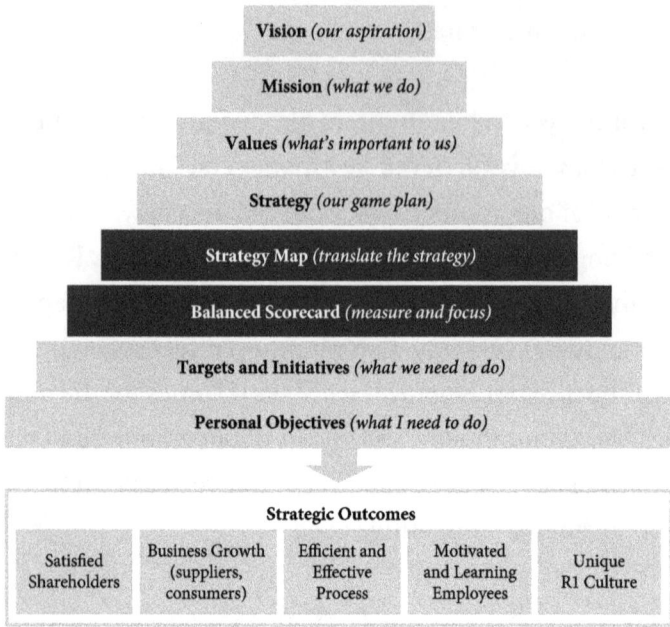

Vision *(our aspiration)*

Mission *(what we do)*

Values *(what's important to us)*

Strategy *(our game plan)*

Strategy Map *(translate the strategy)*

Balanced Scorecard *(measure and focus)*

Targets and Initiatives *(what we need to do)*

Personal Objectives *(what I need to do)*

Strategic Outcomes

Satisfied Shareholders	Business Growth (suppliers, consumers)	Efficient and Effective Process	Motivated and Learning Employees	Unique R1 Culture

R1 International Corporate Strategy Map

Vision: To be the number one global trading company in our field, redefining the industry with responsive solutions and contributing to the greater success of our partners in business.

Mission: Serve, Grow, Prosper

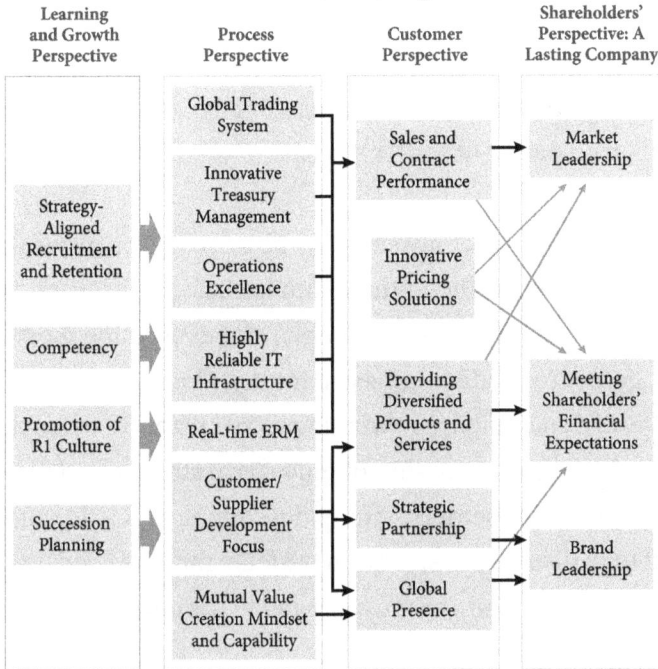

Learning and Growth Perspective	Process Perspective	Customer Perspective	Shareholders' Perspective: A Lasting Company
	Global Trading System	Sales and Contract Performance	Market Leadership
Strategy-Aligned Recruitment and Retention	Innovative Treasury Management		
	Operations Excellence	Innovative Pricing Solutions	
Competency	Highly Reliable IT Infrastructure	Providing Diversified Products and Services	Meeting Shareholders' Financial Expectations
Promotion of R1 Culture	Real-time ERM		
Succession Planning	Customer/ Supplier Development Focus	Strategic Partnership	Brand Leadership
	Mutual Value Creation Mindset and Capability	Global Presence	

ONLY AS STRONG AS OUR WEAKEST LINK

For R1 to function effectively, it's essential that *all* of our teams perform to their highest potential. The distinct aspects of our business are interlinked. If one falters, the entire ship may start to list. We employ four functional teams: the trading team, the operation logistics team, the finance team, and the corporate administrative team. Each one of our locations houses a branch of one of these teams.

The heads of these functional teams combine to forge a fifth team—the group leadership team. This means that leadership figures play a role at each step of a company transaction, whether that's supporting traders during a sale, communicating with the operation logistics team during delivery documentation, or advising the finance team on payment settlement.

The overall R1 family can only be as strong as its weakest link. When the entire chain is strong, all activities and transactions flow smoothly, and everything works together to produce cohesive results. Consider the analogy of a championship-winning soccer team. To triumph, the team must contain not only sharp strikers, but also dynamic midfielders, strong defenders, and a dependable goalkeeper. Everyone on the team must be good, and the winning attitude must permeate the entire team.

Additionally, each person must excel in their specialized role. A defender may not score many goals, but they must be able to make crucial tackles and blocks. It's the same in trading. Traders must be good at selling, while members of the operations team must know how to organize deliveries effectively. They don't need to do each other's jobs, only their own, but they must understand what other team members do.

Additionally, we ensure that we have strong succession

plans in place to cover any eventuality. Each one of our leaders and top managers understands that they must take responsibility for planning their succession so that they don't leave a leadership void when they retire or move elsewhere. Not only should they know who will replace them, they should also know who will move up to fill the position which will be vacated by their successor. This policy operates at every one of R1's twelve locations and differentiates the organization from almost every other. We consider it an essential part of creating and maintaining a strong, motivated, healthy network of leaders.

PEOPLE: R1'S MOST IMPORTANT ASSET

Humans are complex. Managing people isn't as straightforward as managing IT systems. We all have our own sensitivities, and bringing out the best in the people we lead requires a great deal of skill. Both the trading and service industries thrive on the quality, capability, and the attitude of team members, so it's no exaggeration to say that good people must be treasured.

In the early days of R1, it quickly became clear that we needed to establish a strong, resilient corporate culture if the fledgling company was to succeed. When we expanded to become a global virtual company operating in twelve different locations, employing people of several different nationalities, that culture needed to become even stronger. Strong foundations are difficult to build, but easy to break. That's why they must never be taken for granted.

From the outset, we set a goal to create a solid, fulfilling corporate culture that would come to be seen as the best in the industry. We knew that our corporate culture would be absorbed into the very DNA of the company, so we recognized how important it was to get it right from the earliest days of R1's existence.

Looking back, we can say with pride that we've achieved what we set out to do. Our corporate culture has proven both inspiring and robust, delivering sustainable results and making R1 the envy of the company's competitors within the rubber industry.

Everyone who works with R1 knows that they have a responsibility to play their part in shaping corporate culture. They also know that they have the freedom and agency to make good on this responsibility. Our competitors study us and know how we operate. But few are capable of putting in the work to replicate our success. Many people believe that intellectual property is a company's most important asset. At R1, we think differently. We know that it's our people and our culture that give us the edge in a highly competitive industry.

In chapter seven, we'll discuss recent changes in the structure of R1 and tell the story of how the company acquired new shareholders who are powering the company toward even greater growth and success.

New Shareholders

At some point, my time leading R1 will be over. It's important that when I leave, the company continues to thrive and progress. As I've described in other chapters, we have invested consciously in laying a solid foundation for continuous growth since the company's founding in 2001. That platform should enable the company's success to continue long after my retirement.

During our first ten years, we established a network of offices to serve both suppliers and consumers. We provided a wide range of rubber from diverse origins, on flexible trade terms. We sought always to develop business partnerships, not merely to make sales, and to generate fresh solutions for those partners. During that time, R1 became the biggest pure rubber trader in the world.

After our first successful decade, we stopped to ask ourselves what was next. We knew that visionary companies don't stand still; they expand on their successful foundations. Therefore, we wanted to expand and to continue building on the platform we had already established.

It became clear that as margins in the industry continued to diminish, it wasn't feasible for us to continue operating exclusively as a pure rubber trader. While our scope as a trading company was limited, I felt that we had the potential to expand within the rubber value chain. We had the capability, the technology, and the people to enter into the rubber processing business. Furthermore, I had many years of personal experience managing a large processing group, so I knew the business intimately.

Like trading, rubber processing is a margin-management business. Processors purchase rubber from smallholders, convert it, and then sell on the processed rubber. As a company, we were already highly competent in risk management, which gave us a huge advantage as we moved into the rubber processing chain. We could transfer our experience of success in pure rubber trading to the field of rubber processing.

Naturally, there was some trepidation about making such a bold leap. We had a track record of success in pure rubber trading and it would have been easy to rest on our laurels, trusting our existing skills to bring continued success. However, we could see the writing on the wall. Market conditions dictated that the time had come for us to expand the scope of our operations if we wished to see continued growth and prosperity. We also knew that it was in our best interests to take the leap while we still had a strong foundation, solid industry recognition, and overall stability, instead of waiting until prevailing industry trends eroded our core business.

Despite this clarity about our preferred business direction, we lacked a majority stakeholder to lead future growth. Our largest shareholder, with 45 percent, was MARDEC. Cargill held a 25 percent stake, while our remaining investors were companies from Thailand and Indonesia, along with me as a minority shareholder.

Shifting the direction of the company with such a diverse mix of shareholders would have been an unprecedented move. But it soon became apparent that changes were also afoot at Cargill. At the founding of R1, Cargill wished to stay two years, with an option to exit. Ten years later, following an internal restructure, Cargill felt that the time was finally right to leave the rubber trading industry.

Making significant changes to R1's approach required the leadership of a strong, committed majority shareholder with the support of the management team. Where, we wondered, would we find such a shareholder?

With Cargill ready to exit the company, MARDEC expressed interest in filling the vacancy. As an existing shareholder, MARDEC was an obvious choice. The company even had a right of first refusal written into the partnership agreement that had created R1. This meant that if an external company entered a bid to become a majority shareholder, MARDEC had the right to make the acquisition at the same price.

Nonetheless, several members of the board and I had concerns about handing over control of R1 to MARDEC. Previous experience had told us that our vision and theirs weren't always totally in alignment.

Here's an example of what I mean. When we merged the trading operations of MARDEC and Cargill at R1's founding, MARDEC made a commitment to channeling its product through R1. Although it did technically maintain this commitment, its factory managers often looked for ways to deal outside the agreement. To an extent, this was understandable. At times, other companies offered MARDEC superior prices due to prevailing market conditions—or simply in an attempt to outbid us.

During rubber shortages, the pressure was particularly

intense. From our perspective, however, the arrangement was based on a commitment to take MARDEC's product when the price was low, as well as when the price was high, so we objected to MARDEC entertaining other bids when the market was in its favor. The new CEO of MARDEC took the side of the factory managers and ignored his company's commitment to our original agreement. It appeared that he had ideas about making a different arrangement.

When we became aware of the issue, I discussed it with the chairman of MARDEC—who was also the chairman of R1—and with MARDEC's board of directors. All agreed that the company was committed to our agreement, but the chairman lacked the determination to reinforce MARDEC's internal policies and eliminate the friction between the company and R1.

I felt that he was too diplomatic and that he should have taken whatever steps were necessary to resolve the problem, but he hoped to resolve it by being nice. Lacking strong leadership, this tension continued unabated. Factory managers wanted to sell their product to other buyers, while R1's traders were unhappy because they were obliged to take the product during lean times, without the compensation of a guaranteed supply when the market was buoyant.

Predictably, this experience with MARDEC, particularly

with the behavior of its new CEO, sowed doubts in my mind as we discussed the possibility of MARDEC becoming the new majority shareholder of R1. Simultaneously, I considered the possibility of a management buyout, an option I discussed with some of my friends in the banking sector. This wasn't an ideal scenario—I knew that a management buyout would never allow us to fully realize our greater ambitions—but it gave us a fallback option.

If we couldn't find a suitable firm to become a majority shareholder in R1, a management buyout would have allowed us to continue operations. With Cargill leaving, change was inevitable, so I knew I needed to consider all possible scenarios carefully. Nonetheless, I knew that our ideal outcome was to find a powerful entity to act as majority shareholder and allow R1 to expand in accordance with our ambitions.

With the option of a management buyout in my back pocket, I informed the board that we had two other interested parties, in addition to MARDEC. They asked me to send them official, concrete expressions of interest, including offers, terms, and details. The two outside parties followed this protocol, submitting their bids to the shareholders.

For me, it was a time of excitement and anxiety. As the company's founder, I felt a great responsibility to ensure that R1 was delivered to the right hands. I was emotionally attached to the company, and it was vital to me that any new majority shareholder take R1 to the next level. I was confident that R1 had the foundations to reach greater heights, but the company had to be in the right hands. For this reason, I sat down to outline some key expectations of potential new majority shareholders.

The new party had to understand a great deal about the commodity industry, preferably specializing in rubber. They had to understand the cyclical nature of commodity trade and respect the need for long-term focus. I knew that a company expecting immediate gratification, without the stamina to stay the course during difficult times, would be a poor fit for R1.

A new majority shareholder had to also be financially sound and willing to invest in the company's future. The rubber industry contains many competitors, some of whom have enormous financial reach. At the time this transition was taking place, industry changes were turning some of our larger competitors into superpowers—one of the reasons why a management buyout felt like a step backwards.

We didn't need a new shareholder that would simply replace MARDEC. It was important that whoever took over offered R1 fresh and distinct possibilities. We wanted a shareholder that recognized R1's existing strengths, while simultaneously seeing the potential for the company to become even bigger and better. We were looking for ambition, determination, and a willingness to channel those qualities into the R1 brand and platform.

In addition, it was essential that any new majority shareholder continued to value the corporate culture R1 had built up over the years. As discussed in the previous chapter, we understand how crucial a motivated and responsible workforce is to R1's success. We wanted our new majority shareholder to respect this commitment to employee fulfillment. Without it, we knew that we ran the risk of losing key people and declining from our preeminent position in the market.

I presented these criteria to the board, explaining that I felt using them as a guide would help us to evaluate candidates objectively and make a decision that was in the company's best interests. Fortunately, the right candidate was already on our radar.

MAKING A DEAL

Of the two interested parties who made representations to the board, one was a state-owned Chinese rubber company named Hainan State Farm/Hainan Rubber Group

(HSF-HRG). The other was a very large, reputable agricultural commodity company listed in Singapore.

Based in Hainan, China, HSF-HRG wanted to acquire a reputable global trading company to use as a springboard for its international operations. Before meeting with us, the company's CEO had toured Singapore, meeting with a number of rubber veterans to determine which was the biggest and best rubber trading company in the region. He received a unanimous answer: R1.

Naturally, his next step was to arrange a meeting with me. I sat down with him and another veteran of the industry, and he explained the company's interest. At the time, I knew little about its background and I was unfamiliar with the company's CEO and leadership team. The interpreter who arrived with the CEO was excellent but, nonetheless, communicating through a third party reduced my comfort level.

In addition, it would be fair to say that Chinese companies were often perceived negatively in Singapore in this period. The popular belief was that their governance, outlook, and operations fell short of the standards I required to consider them as potential majority shareholders. Taking all these factors into account, I was skeptical. I found it hard to believe that HSF-HRG was the right company to purchase R1.

Despite my misgivings, however, the company's CEO returned to meet with me again. Prior to this second meeting, I did some research and spoke to some friends who understood the Chinese rubber industry. I discovered that HSF had been established in 1982 as a state-owned enterprise by the Hainan provincial government. The company employed approximately two hundred thousand people, an enormous number, and owned more than ten million acres of land in Hainan, much of which was used to grow rubber, tropical fruits, and vegetables.

HRG was founded in 2005, specifically to handle the rubber branch of HSF's business. By 2011, it was listed on the Shanghai Stock Exchange, becoming the largest agricultural stock on the exchange. HRG owned 235,000 hectares of land and boasted a production capacity of 400,000 tons a year. These numbers constituted the single largest rubber plantation in the world, with thirteen rubber processing factories and sixteen subsidiary companies in logistics and warehousing. HRG alone employed sixty thousand people. When I understood the scale of HSF-HRG's operations, I was shocked.

In terms of reach and ambition, it was clear that HSF-HRG not only met my expectations, it surpassed them. Nonetheless, I still nursed some concerns. Even under the ownership of a new majority shareholder, I wanted R1 to remain independent and operate professionally. Also, I wanted to protect our existing structures of global governance and the corporate culture we had worked so hard to develop.

The second meeting ran much more smoothly than the first. The CEO seemed to understand my desire to treat employees well and reward key managers for their long service and loyalty. HSF-HRG proposed that key members of the management team—who at the time weren't shareholders—could purchase company equity up to a combined maximum of 10 percent. This was a very unusual offer, intended to motivate important personnel to remain in situ, and I felt it reflected an understanding of the value of these people to the company.

HSF-HRG and I also discussed my own personal shareholding. Before negotiations, I held a 5 percent stake in R1, with an option to increase my holding up to 14 percent. HSF understood that my influence had shaped the company and that it wouldn't be interested in purchasing it without the time I had invested in R1 over the years. So, when HSF acquired R1, the company's leaders invited me to purchase an additional 5 percent stake, increasing my total holdings to 10 percent.

The CEO reassured me further by giving me a mandate to prepare R1 for a possible listing on the Singapore Stock Exchange. To go public, I knew that R1 would need to meet strict regulatory standards, operating professionally and demonstrating compliance with the requirements of a listed company.

When HSF-HRG offered to incentivize R1's employees, invited me to acquire an increased stake, and made plans to list the company on the Singapore Stock Exchange, I began to trust that the group was serious about putting in place structures that ensured the long-term health of the company we had built from the ground up. Nonetheless, the other external company also gave us a firm offer, and both proposals were attractive.

Before the board and I could come to a decision, we needed to discuss the relative merits of both proposals. Both offers were well above the expectations of the shareholders. Eventually, we decided that HSF-HRG's plan to expand its international reach gave it the edge. It was also superior in financial terms, as well as more conducive to our management approach.

MARDEC, however, still had right of first refusal. If the company wished, it could match HSF-HRG's offer and become the majority shareholder of R1. It was a nervous time for those of us who had concerns about handing R1 to MARDEC, so we were understandably relieved when the company withdrew its interest and agreed to continue to sell to the new buyer under similar terms.

All the original shareholders disposed of their shares to HSF-HRG and exited the company, making a very handsome return on the deal. On April 28, 2012, R1 came under new ownership. HSF took a 60 percent stake, with HRG claiming 15 percent. Twenty-three key management employees shared 10 percent between them and I held 10 percent. Our Thai shareholder, meanwhile, decided to buy back into the company, taking a 5 percent stake.

When we sought new shareholders, we knew that it was essential that we found the right fit. We wanted owners with strong motivation to sustain the growth and excellence that had characterized R1's first decade. We also knew it was essential that our new majority shareholders respected the people who worked at R1, and that they were willing to build a relationship based on trust and commitment. In short, we wanted shareholders who were committed to the success and development of our employees. In HSF-HRG, we found that partner.

With the deal signed, a new era dawned for R1. I felt extremely proud of how we handled the transition, navigating what could have been a tricky situation with aplomb and ultimately securing the right people—with the right vision—to take R1 forward. In the following chapter, we'll cover the next phase of R1's growth.

CHAPTER EIGHT

Prospering Worldwide

In the first fifteen years of R1's existence, from 2001 to 2016, our group turnover of total physical rubber business was $18.3 billion. This amounted to an annual average of $1.22 billion, although, due to rubber price fluctuation, it varied significantly. In some years our turnover topped $3 billion. This level of revenue turnover has secured us access to some valuable benefits, including an attractive variable taxation rate.

Physical Rubber Turnover Growth

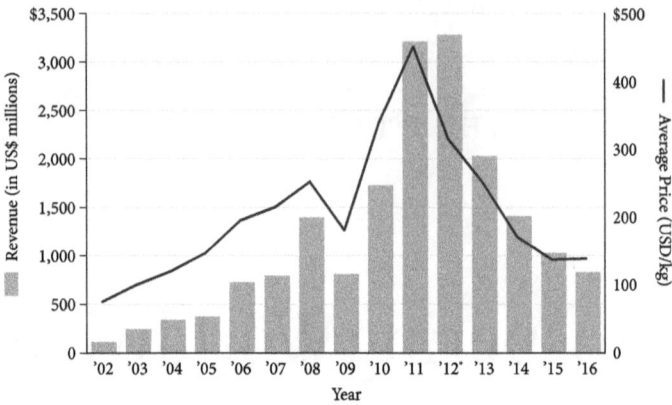

- Total turnover over the fifteen years of operation was US $18.3 billion and the annual average turnover was US $1.22 billion
- Influenced by rubber prices
* Year 2012: fifteen months of operation

At the end of 2016, the net tangible, or book value, of the company was $68.5 million. Our annual return on equity was 12 percent to 49 percent, with an average of 24 percent. No one came close to these sterling results in the world of rubber trading.

Net Tangible Assets

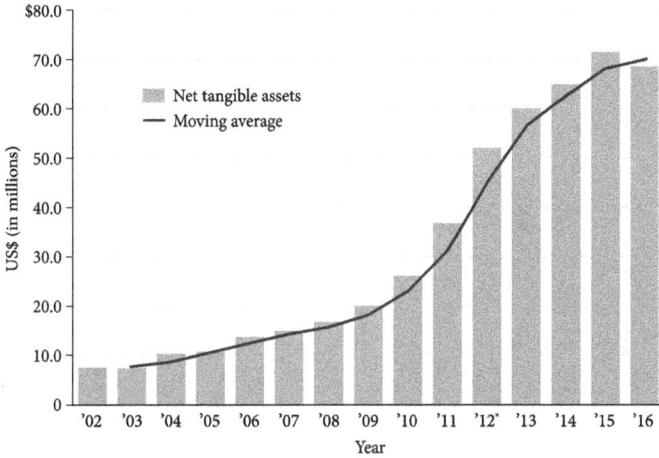

* Year 2012: fifteen months of operation

Return on Equity

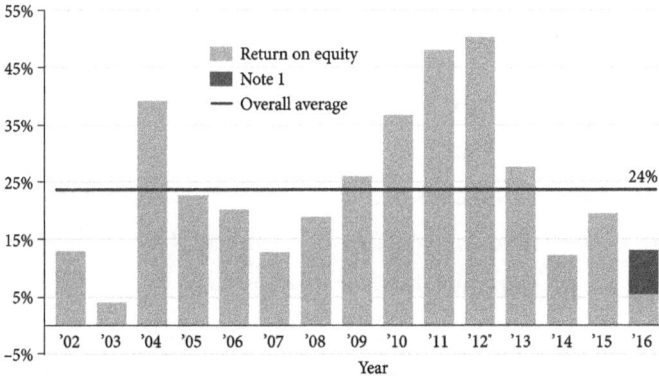

Note 1: *In 2016, the group incurred an unusual expense relating to the arbitration, amounting to US $2.2 million. The group also ventured into the processing business, which incurred start-up costs/losses of US $2.3 million.*

• Overall average ROE over fifteen years of operation was 24 percent
* Year 2012: fifteen months of operation

Return on equity (ROE) is a measure of profitability that calculates how many dollars of profit a company generates with each dollar of shareholders' equity.

During those fifteen years, we moved 17.4 million tons of rubber across both fiscal and futures markets, averaging 1.2 million tons a year. These numbers make us the largest pure rubber trader in the world.

Total Volume Growth: Physical and Futures

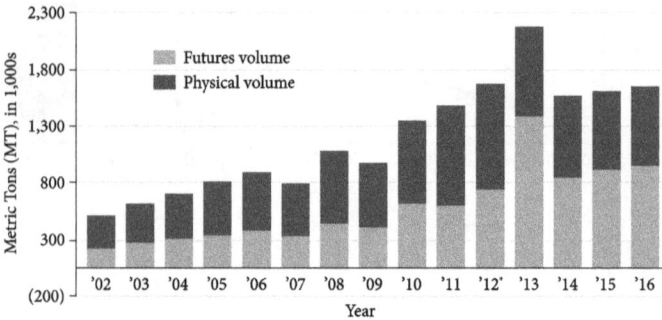

- Total volume over fifteen years of operation was 17.4 million MT, while average volume was 1.2 million MT per annum
* Year 2012: fifteen months of operation

Naturally, we're exceptionally proud of all these achievements, although perhaps the one we're most proud of is the financial success achieved by our shareholders. In 2001, they invested a total of $7 million. Over a decade and a half, that initial investment grew to $113.7 million, more than sixteen times the original seed capital. To 2016, we have paid out a total of $30.5 million to shareholders, with an average dividend of 7.7 percent per year, and one-time dividends of up to 19 percent.

Total Business Return Growth

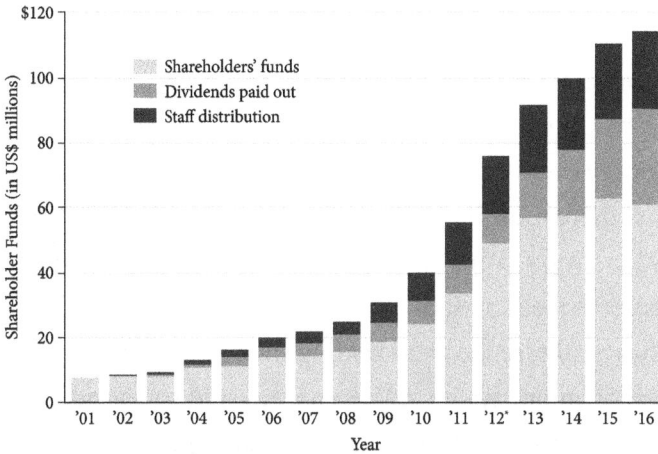

Shareholder Funds (in US$ millions)

Legend:
- Shareholders' funds
- Dividends paid out
- Staff distribution

- Shareholders' fund has grown substantially since the commencement of operation in 2001, from US $7 million to US $113.7 million, i.e. more than 16.2 times its initial seed capital
* Year 2012: fifteen months of operation

These numbers demonstrate R1's unequalled prosperity and consistency. In the cyclical commodity industry, rubber trading companies generally find it extraordinarily difficult to generate consistent profits. Normally, they perform well for a number of years, then experience years of loss. For R1 to maintain profit consistently and pay dividends of 7 percent each year is an achievement unparalleled in the rubber industry.

Based on our achievements and high turnover, R1 has been recognized as one of the top two hundred companies in Singapore, a huge accomplishment. This recognition opened the door to the Global Trader Program, an honor accorded by International Enterprise, the agency of the Ministry of Trade in Singapore.

Many people in the industry have expressed curiosity about how we accomplished these numbers, thinking that there must be some magic to our success. The truth is far simpler: our strengths lie in our platform, in our experienced traders, and in our discipline. We have always adhered to clear trading strategies guided by risk management systems. We have enjoyed strong support from shareholders, bankers, and our highly progressive corporate council.

SHARED SUCCESS

All R1 stakeholders, from shareholders, suppliers, and buyers to employees—and even the rubber industry itself—have benefited from our success. MARDEC, Cargill, and the other shareholders who sold their stakes each received a total return on seed capital of 847 percent. MARDEC invested $3.15 million, which yielded a gain of $26.695 million. Cargill invested $1.75 million, reaping a gain of $14.83 million. When HSF-HRG publicly announced in 2012 that it had acquired the company, prices jumped so much that the rise in the market exceeded the total cost of its purchase. Overall, HSF-HRG has succeeded in recovering half of its investment within five years of its acquisition.

When HSF-HRG bought R1, we were serving 2,200 customers in nearly eighty countries as a one-stop trading center where customers could purchase different grades of rubber from different origins. Fortunately, the sale did nothing to disrupt the smooth running of those transactions. On the contrary, it was appreciated by both our customers and suppliers, whom we always considered our partners in business. They felt that the acquisition represented a guarantee of the same high level of service with which they were familiar, with great potential for further sustainable growth. In consequence, these buyers and suppliers have maintained their loyalty to us, and their growth, in turn, has continued.

As a pure rubber trading company, we have never sought involvement at the level of the farm gate. Factory representatives may meet with farmers, but pure rubber traders do not. In the early days of my career, I dealt regularly with farmers, so I always felt conflicted about the lack of opportunity we had to communicate with them directly. In 2012, however, we had the opportunity to renew our involvement with the rubber farming community.

R1 India, our Indian company, formed an association with a cooperative society named Mendipathar Society. Mendipathar Society operated in northeastern India, a poor, mountainous tribal area new to the rubber-grade market. Assisted by Sister Rose, a Catholic nun with a desire to improve the lives of poor farmers, we struck up a commitment to liberating the farmers from the clutches of greedy money lenders. We did this by educating them on the importance of producing high-quality rubber, then purchasing that rubber from them at a fair market price.

Until we intervened, it was hard for the farmers to negotiate a fair price for their wares, which the market viewed as a new product of unknown quality. When our traders in India took their rubber and their story to some of the big manufacturers of tires and other rubber products in the country, we succeeded in convincing those companies to purchase the farmers' rubber via R1. We helped them improve the quality of their product, negotiate a fair price, and supply their rubber to consumers. In this way, we succeeded in helping them to improve their standard of living.

Since we began this partnership in 2012, this Indian society has seen excellent growth. It has even established four new branches, employing approximately one hundred employees in the field of operations. This initiative, which has allowed a deserving community to grow and prosper, has also inspired our employees to focus on other projects they can support in the future. This has been an incredibly satisfying project for everyone involved. Not only have our shareholders, partners, and employees benefited from R1's activities, communities in need have also reaped rewards.

Members of the R1 global family, spread across nine different countries, have benefited significantly from the company's prosperity. As described in the previous chapter, twenty-three members of key management became shareholders in 2012, giving them skin in the game and enhanced motivation to contribute to R1's success. Between 2001 and 2016, we have shared $24 million of profits with R1's employees. In good years, some of our key managers have enjoyed more than twenty-four months of their salary as bonus payments, a level of remuneration that has allowed them to achieve financial freedom. A few have become millionaires, while almost every member of staff has succeeded in improving their overall standard of living. Many have purchased houses and better cars, and they have sent their children to excellent private schools.

R1's financial growth has allowed all of us to prosper. More importantly, however, our team members have experienced tremendous personal and professional growth over the years. This has led to immense personal satisfaction, a reward more valuable than any financial dividend. We feel that our strategy of employing the best, rewarding them generously, and motivating them to grow continuously has more than justified itself over the years.

GIVING BACK TO THE INDUSTRY

While we all wish to enjoy a high standard of living, it's always been important to us that we're not selfish. We know that our success depends on the success of others, so we make an effort to support the industry as a whole. Our key managers and global offices have been actively involved in trade associations over the years and have served on countless trade bodies. Our trading heads in Japan, the United States, Malaysia, Thailand, Vietnam, India, China, and Singapore all play an active role in their country's trade association, contributing selflessly to the industry as a whole.

Personally, I've spent a lot of time working with rubber associations, as well as providing advisory services and support to various domestic and international rubber agencies. For many years, I have taken an active leadership role in the International Rubber Study Group (IRSG), serving as the chairman of both its Statistical Committee and Economic Committee, along with its International Advisory Panel (IAP). In addition, I have long been an active member of the International Rubber Association (IRA) Management Committee. I also served as the chairman of SICOM, the rubber committee of the Singapore Stock Exchange.

When it became necessary for IRSG to move its headquarters from the United Kingdom, I campaigned actively for a relocation to Singapore, which is the zenith for all major rubber-producing and consuming countries, as well as a global trading hub through which more than 70 percent of world rubber trade passes. As a responsible member of the industry, we believe that we have a duty to contribute positively to the development of a healthy and progressive rubber industry.

For a company to stand the test of time, *all* stakeholders must benefit. Ultimately, our success can only be measured by our contribution to the industry as a whole. I've never measured R1's success by how much I've personally benefited; instead, our shared success can be measured by the recognition we receive throughout the industry. Individually, we all need to feel that our lives are meaningful. Collectively, when we come together to form a company, we must trust that it has a purpose beyond personal enrichment. We must feel that we are part of something greater than ourselves, making a contribution to others and making the world a better place. The ninth and tenth chapters of this book will explore the current and future state of the rubber industry, along with R1's part in creating a business environment that serves *all* stakeholders.

CHAPTER NINE

New Dawn for Sustained Success

Over the course of fifteen years of R1's existence, we have exerted a painstaking effort to build a strong foundation and pursue our mission to serve, grow, and prosper. When the time came to hand over the reins of the company to new shareholders, we were confident that this foundation would provide the platform for a quantum leap into the future.

To reiterate, the fundamental aspects of our success are numerous. Our effective corporate structure includes twelve offices in key rubber-producing and consuming countries. Our cohesive, focused, and dynamic global family consists of the best talent in the rubber industry. Every one of R1's global heads is experienced, hardworking, and passionate about rubber. Our teams may be dispersed across several different time zones, but they are all united by our common vision and operate as a single virtual family. Technologically speaking, our group is connected via an online platform, which we update constantly. When we partnered with Cargill, we inherited an advanced risk management system. Over time, we fine-tuned that system so that it fit our needs precisely.

Another building block of our success has been our unique strategic management culture. This provides us with a method of assessing—and sharing—the company's employee self-esteem and motivation levels. We formed this platform on the values of accountability, responsibility, teamwork, innovation, integrity, and trust. It has always been important to us that we cater to the personal and professional goals of our team members, that they have fun at work, and that they enjoy what they do.

We've always emphasized the importance of discipline, a vital component of a successful trading company. Our exemplary corporate governance is based on strategic discipline, a norm that has become second nature to everyone in the group. This disciplined approach to trading feeds a strong relationship with the banks that support our activities, allowing us to finance our growth and expansion.

I'm proud of the fact that we employ a solid pool of young, talented traders with many years of accumulated industry knowledge, experience, and recognition. We hire them, train them, develop them, and they stay with us because they are passionate about the industry and they like working with R1. In addition, our three-level succession planning, applicable to each one of our key leadership positions, gives them a clear understanding of how their careers can progress.

GUIDED BY OUR VALUES

Over a decade and a half, our culture of shared values has made us a universally recognized, trusted brand in the global rubber trade. This brand means a lot to us—it's impossible to put a monetary worth on a system of values, but it means a lot to our buyers, our suppliers, and to us.

Our values are ingrained in our corporate culture. They guide us in representing our company and demonstrate our uniqueness and difference. Many people wish they could emulate us, but because values are so intangible, it's difficult for them to replicate our success in their own organizations. For us, R1's corporate culture is like our own treasured corporate culture.

We have become the only company in the industry recognized as a one-stop trading center. This means that we are capable of handling procurement from fourteen rubber-producing countries in Asia and Africa. Wherever rubber is grown, we can procure the material. This exceptional reach allows us to offer more than twenty different types and qualities of rubber to our customers. We are able to supply any quantity our customers require and offer a fixed price far into the future.

Throughout the years, we've formed relationships with 2,200 rubber suppliers. We have networks of buyers in 70 countries and 150 ports. This is the global platform that our new shareholders inherited when they purchased R1.

SHAREHOLDER RESTRUCTURING SINCE 2012

When HSF-HRG purchased a majority stake in R1 in 2012, it gave me and the rest of the management team a mandate to list the business on the Singapore Stock Exchange. This was a task that we approached with great enthusiasm, working to expand the business and its profitability and further improving systems and processes to conform to the requirements for listing a public company in Singapore. Initially, we were confident that we would succeed in listing R1 on the Singapore Stock Exchange in March 2015. We appointed the issue manager, the legal team, the auditors, the financial advisors, and the consultants. We also completed a draft IPO prospectus, consisting of an independent report.

Unfortunately, the IPO process hit a wall. We encountered a conflict of interest. It transpired that HRG owned another office involved in the rubber trading business in Singapore; this firm was similar to R1, although it operated on a smaller scale. Unfortunately, HRG Singapore—a subsidiary of the parent company listed in Shanghai—could not agree to close its Singapore operation and resolve this conflict of interest. Without a resolution, we would not have been able to secure approval to list R1 on the Singapore Stock Exchange. Despite our efforts, it looked as though we would be unable to take the final step toward floating the company publicly.

As the majority shareholder and the party responsible for delivering a mandate to list R1, HSF-HRG was naturally motivated to find a fair solution. We discussed a variety of options, but it wasn't possible to settle on one. The situation was complicated by the fact that, at this time, both HSF and HRG were undergoing major structural changes, with new personnel taking over at the top. In a short space of time, both companies appointed both a new chairman and a new CEO. Suddenly, the people we had worked with from day one vacated their positions, giving way to new faces.

Nonetheless, we continued to discuss the situation with the new leaders of the company, who were genuine and cooperative in their efforts to reach a new solution. Eventually, we found a plan that worked. HSF proposed selling its entire stake in R1 to HRG. Simultaneously, all of our key management personnel and myself would do likewise—an option that made sense for us when it became apparent that we would not succeed in listing R1, because that scenario closed off the possibility of a profitable exit. Instead, we could exit at the book value of the company, based on independently audited 2017 financial numbers. Those who remained part of the company and continued to work for R1 would be offered new employment terms and special benefits. The company itself would become a wholly owned subsidiary of HRG Shanghai.

Under the circumstances, this solution made the best sense. By 2016, R1 could not remain a pure trading company and succeed in a marketplace populated by newer, stronger competitors. Meanwhile, HRG was already restructuring various business ventures and activities. The company's leadership wished to focus all their rubber activity in areas where they were substantial shareholders, and acquiring R1 completely gave them a footing to do that with the company. When we agreed to the deal, we trusted that HRG wanted to build on the foundation of R1.

The arrangement worked for everyone involved. HRG inherited the legacy and strength of R1, which helped it to realize its own ambitious plans to become a leading global conglomerate. For R1's minority shareholders, with the option of a profitable exit at a later date closed off to us, the value of being a minority partner in a private company diminished. Therefore, it made sense to sell our holdings in R1.

The move also made sense for the company as a whole. This internal restructuring and HRG's resulting owner-ship placed R1 in a highly beneficial position. HRG is located in China, the world's largest rubber market. It has a strong pedigree, coupled with the financial might to capitalize on the R1 platform and engage profitably in many aspects of the rubber trade, from plantation, pro-cessing, and trading to supply chain management and the manufacture of rubber products. At a later date, HRG may decide to move into other related products, such as syn-thetic rubber, rubber chemicals, and rubber technologies.

Initially, failing to list R1 on the Singapore Stock Exchange was a big disappointment. As a subsidiary of HRG, how-ever, the company can become part of a formidable global rubber conglomerate. The acquisition of R1 by HRG will move us closer to our goal of becoming the number one rubber company in the entire world.

Ultimately, I believe that HRG has the potential to handle 25 percent to 30 percent of rubber production and sales throughout the world. As I write these words, I am leading the HSF-HRG team engaged in negotiations to buy into Kirana Megatara, the biggest rubber producer in Indonesia. We are also pursuing other acquisition opportunities in Thailand, Malaysia, Vietnam, and Africa. For example, the company is investigating the possibility of purchasing major rubber products manufacturing companies and a specialized latex company.

As the founder of R1, I'm highly encouraged by this dynamic approach. The leaders of HSF and HRG act in concert, recognizing their potential to become a major force in the industry. Between their strong leadership and wealth of resources, I'm convinced that they will achieve the goals I had in mind when I first conceived the idea of R1. I know that the company I founded is in the right hands, and I am excited about what lies ahead. With the leadership of HRG, we'll be able to reach heights that we couldn't have attained alone. The future looks rosy indeed.

CHAPTER TEN

The Future of the Rubber Industry

When we founded R1 in 2001, the dominant mood in the rubber industry was despondency and complacency. At the time, rubber prices stood at $450 per ton—a record low. This price was so low that rubber farmers faced serious hardship. In many rubber-producing countries, the issue spilled into the political sphere, with angry farmers protesting to their governments. The leaders of their countries were looking desperately for ways to help smallholders.

Many pundits believed at the time that the rubber industry had become a sunset industry, doomed to suffer a slow decline. Bucking this trend, I believed that the industry would turn around and that a better future lay ahead. I felt that the time was right for a progressive rubber trading company to enter the market, a company that would redefine the industry by serving direct needs and forging mutually beneficial partnerships with both suppliers and customers. Despite the cards stacked against us, we were determined to enter the industry and claim leadership.

R1 began with a clear vision: to redefine the rubber industry by delivering strong customer solutions and making a greater contribution to the success of our partners. In the process, our goal was to become the number one global rubber trading company. The mission was simple, clear, and revolutionary: to serve, grow, and prosper.

Over time, we have achieved commendable success on the back of our vision and values. As of 2016, we have a proven track record of steady performance, along with a global platform—the stewardship of HRG—that will propel us toward our next quantum leap.

Rubber is now a mature industry, with more than 150 years of history. Nonetheless, industry leaders cannot afford to rest on their laurels. There are many changes and challenges on the horizon. As an individual company, too, R1 must always continue to evolve and resist the temptation to rely on the glory of its past. We must always remain mindful of market conditions so that we avoid potential pitfalls and seize the opportunities that open up for us.

Given the nature of the industry, there will always be a need for entrepreneurial, transformational, and inspiring leadership. A strong leader must assemble the right teams, motivate them effectively, and create a solid yet flexible corporate structure. A successful leader must also adopt the best available processes and systems, persevere in the face of challenges, and inspire team members with their passion. Above all, a leader must operate with clear vision and find ways to bring everyone they work with into alignment with that vision.

TRENDS ON THE HORIZON

Specifically, there are several trends on the horizon with the potential to seriously disrupt our industry. The first is that rubber faces a potential production surplus. Over the years, world rubber supply and demand have been broadly in balance. In 2011, however, driven by China's double-digit growth, rubber prices shot up to almost $6,000 per ton. Economists forecast that prices could reach as high as $8,000 per ton. This, combined with a rise in crude oil prices to $147 per barrel, sparked a euphoric reaction and created the impetus for increased rubber production.

Some of that increase took place in established Asian rubber-producing countries. Thailand, Indonesia, Vietnam, Cambodia, Myanmar, and Laos began growing more rubber. Some came from African countries, such as Cameroon, Ghana, and the Ivory Coast. Ironically, this rise in production could ultimately prove harmful to the rubber industry. Despite this growth in production capacity, analysts do not anticipate a large growth in rubber demand. All the indications are that rubber demand will continue to grow, but only gradually.

In addition to the growth in productive land dedicated to rubber, advances in breeding have created trees that can yield three times as much rubber as current varieties. This is more than a minor bump—it has the potential to generate a huge surplus in world rubber production, making a lasting impact on the industry. Some experts believe that, by 2025, total world rubber production could reach nineteen million tons per annum, with projected demand peaking at seventeen million tons per annum. Should this happen, there will be a huge surplus of two million tons per annum, a situation which would have dire consequences for rubber producers.

Yet we could avoid this surplus if we start to make fuller use of the products of rubber trees. For decades now, rubber scientists have known that the rubber tree is a multidimensional factory, whose products have many applications. For example, extracts from the tree can be used in some pharmaceutical products.

Despite the tree's potential, however, there have been no major breakthroughs in determining substantial new uses for rubber products. Although there have been a few small discoveries, they have not had a substantial impact on rates of rubber consumption. No concerted research has yet been undertaken to discover new uses for rubber. As of 2018, nearly 70 percent of rubber is used in the automobile and tire industry alone.

Recent developments suggest that the greatest potential use of rubber could lie in road construction. With millions of kilometers of roadway constructed around the world every year, imagine the possibilities for the industry if rubber became a significant component. This alone could consume much of the rubber industry's growing surplus.

We've yet to see tangible efforts on this front, but I believe that rubber-producing countries in Southeast Asia, along with China and India, should take the bold step of mandating that all roads *must* make rubber an important component of their construction. This would have benefits both for the industry and for road users; roads that include a percentage of rubber would be smoother and longer lasting than pure tarmac constructions, requiring minimal maintenance.

It may seem that incorporating rubber into all road construction is a major step, but it can be easily achieved with the political will to make a positive change. Certainly, it would be far more effective than typical government measures to counter a surfeit of rubber in the market, which mainly involve intervening to buy back rubber stock and withhold it from the market or imposing import/export quotas.

Another threat to rubber consumption is developments in the automobile industry that are reducing the weight and prolonging the life of tires. Technologically advanced tires, coupled with AI, will lead to higher mileage per tire. Sensors within tires will lead to optimal inflation and maximize lifespan. This trend favors long-lasting tires, resulting in reduced demand for rubber.

The prognosis continues to look bad. Breakthrough developments in synthetic rubber, using biomass-generated monomers which yield polymers of equal or higher quality than natural rubber, may start to overtake existing rubber products. Bridgestone has recently reported the development of a new variety of synthetic rubber made from ethylene, butadiene, and isoprene. The manufacturers claim that this product delivers vastly improved performance in comparison with natural rubber.

An emphasis on industry sustainability could see

increased usage of regenerated rubber, recycled rubber, and retreading, another trend which will lengthen the life-cycle of tires and reduce demand for new rubber. China has already reported four million metric tons of installed capacity for reprocessing previously used rubber. In the United States, Michelin's purchase of Lehigh Technologies confirms the interest of the big players in exploring this route. Recycled plastic is beginning to replace rubber in some applications, for example in shoes.

Additionally, consumer behavior is changing. Electric vehicles are becoming significantly more popular, a trend which will certainly have an impact on the design of future wheels and tires. With 95 percent of cars parked at any given moment, car-sharing services and ride-ordering apps such as Uber and Grab are already making it viable for people to decide against purchasing vehicles outright. In urban areas, rented communal bicycles and electric stand-on scooters are replacing cars over short distances. Advanced research in flying cars and flying suits point toward a future in which the need for rubber might be substantially reduced.

Some of these trends may seem a long way from coming to fruition. Some may even appear far-fetched. For rubber producers, however, they could be highly damaging. You may wonder why the potential decline of rubber matters. Industries come and go all the time. As a veteran of the rubber industry, I am naturally emotionally attached to it, but I'm also concerned for the smallholders who grow most of the rubber produced in the world. For them, growing rubber is a magnificent way to eliminate poverty.

A tree takes six to seven years to reach maturity. Once they begin to yield, rubber trees can be tapped for approximately twenty-five years. For a small farmer, a rubber tree is like an ATM machine, as long as the market is sufficiently buoyant to provide the farmer with a fair price. Should the market collapse, millions of people in rubber-producing countries will be impoverished. Additionally, rubber trees absorb carbon dioxide, mitigating the impact of climate change.

If the rubber market is to avoid saturation, we must urgently and seriously seek ways of creating new demand for surplus rubber. Without this change, we can expect to see prices decrease steadily as the gap between supply and demand grows, which is our third industry trend. In rubber-producing countries, the livelihoods of millions of people depend on the value of rubber. If prices fall, those farmers may agitate for government regulation of prices.

This has happened previously. While I was writing this book, prices dipped to approximately $1,200 per ton, a rate that falls below the cost of production in many producing countries. Compare this price with the $3,000 to $6,000 per ton achieved in previous years, and you see how much the income of rubber producers has fallen.

This trend is compounded by other realities of the rubber industry. Many rubber farmers are older than sixty—it's not a popular trade for young people. To do their work, they resort to employing temporary help. When rubber prices are low, they find it difficult to afford external help.

Over the past century, smallholders have typically borne the brunt of periods of low and depressed rubber prices. To address this concern and attract new people to the industry, I feel that it is necessary for the government to make a holistic intervention. In the past, governments have supported measures that brought smallholders temporary relief.

Despite these efforts, however, no government has created meaningful long-term measures to address the hardships sustained by smallholders when prices are low. We need to see more serious, long-term measures to address the conditions of the market, not merely through artificially raising prices but, for example, by mandating the use of rubber in roads, a step that could boost the entire rubber market at a stroke. Additionally, smallholders should be encouraged and assisted, both to diversify their rubber land use by growing other cash crops or rearing poultry and to get involved in other small business activities that can augment their income.

Western governments and other bodies, such as the European Commission, automotive manufacturers, and NGOs, are increasingly seeking to add pressure with the demands of green labeling and sustainability certification. This leads us to the fourth major industry trend: demand for higher-quality rubber and sustainable practices.

These practices encompass all facets of the industry, from production standards to environmental impact. Sustainable rubber is farmed with concern for the people who grow it and the social and ecological consequences of its production. For example, EU standards require workers to receive fair wages and outlaw child labor. They insist that rubber is grown without creating pollution or destroying forests, and they set minimum standards of employee welfare. This trend, while positive in many ways, may place additional pressure on those producers who are already suffering from slim margins and depressed prices. Any meaningful definition of sustainability must include responsible partnership, with a focus on the growth and prosperity of all stakeholders.

The trading landscape is changing rapidly as well. Many traders have resorted to taking higher trading risks, and even to speculation, simply to stay in business. To earn money, they employ trading strategies such as directional trades and spread trades. With opportunities few and far between, even this may not be enough to keep them in business. Large consolidated entities are usurping fragmented owner-operators, using their greater financial power to achieve economies of scale. Their size allows them to look at the industry strategically, instead of viewing it purely as an arena for immediate gains.

This fifth trend also includes a shift to China. The dominant futures market, which is not currently open to foreign participants, is now in Shanghai. On some days, the volume of daily futures contracts in China exceeds annual global production of rubber. Traditional global rubber traders do not have access to the most liquid market, and they're unable to read the market clearly because of its speculative nature. The firms participating in the Shanghai market are very different players from the traditional rubber traders. Commodity funds and speculative investors dominate the market. Unless traditional rubber traders can adapt to this shift, they may soon go extinct.

We may soon witness the end of the era when family-owned and operated rubber companies were viable players in the industry, as they are forced to give way to larger and stronger players that are involved in the entire value chain. Eventually, it seems likely that only a few large, bold, financially strong entities will survive, those willing and able to take a long-term view of the industry. Unless family-owned rubber companies are willing to take a more strategic approach to their business, they'll be pushed out, primarily by the financially powerful Chinese companies which are entering the market.

NEW OPPORTUNITIES FOR STAKEHOLDERS

While the picture may appear bleak, there are nonetheless opportunities available in this changing landscape for businesses to understand the direction of the industry and plan for the future. Sustaining the status quo is not an option. Companies cannot afford to neglect the evolving demands of the market and stay in business. At R1, we know this well. We're keenly aware that we must constantly build on our success, and that we must continually reinvent and revitalize ourselves to remain part of the industry. Companies that refuse to take these steps run the risk of becoming irrelevant, ignored, and unsustainable.

On a positive note, I anticipate that a closer connection will develop between stakeholders such as rubber suppliers, farmers, and end users. In time, I believe this will result in an improved relationship between rubber producers and consumers.

Right now, most stakeholders operate within their individual silos. Most have taken few—if any—steps toward forging a more complementary relationship with one another. There are various intergovernmental and international agencies, such as the International Rubber Study Group, which exist to provide a forum where all stakeholders in the rubber industry can come together to discuss common industry trends and issues. For most players, however, it's easy to forget that the consumer and the producer are two sides of the same coin. Even though all parties have the same goal in mind, unfortunately the rubber industry is an environment where the relationship between stakeholders is often riven with conflict and tension. With the development of stronger conglomerates and larger professional groups, this will surely change, generating a healthier rubber industry.

Major players in the industry must understand that their business derives from the smallholders. Smallholders are a critical part of the business who deserve more attention than they currently receive. Until recently, the industry has been so fragmented that the needs of smallholders have slipped through the cracks. Most consumers have dealt only with traders.

The rubber industry of the future must look beyond the immediate commercial objective. Companies must consider the smallholder a critical element of their business.

Smallholders must produce quality rubber using sustainable methods; in return, they must be paid a fair price and supported during difficult times.

R1 and HRG are in a good place to encounter an ever-changing industry landscape with optimism. Within the next five to ten years, I believe that the rubber industry I've known for more than forty years will change radically. Stronger conglomerates, with a more developed focus on technology and innovative products, will rule the industry. The entire value chain will play a role in moving rubber, while supply chain management will be key.

I'm excited for the future of both R1 and HRG. Together, we have the potential to become a dominant player in the rubber industry of the future. In fact, as part of our global expansion strategy, we have already started the process of acquiring the largest rubber processing group in Indonesia. We're also in talks with other leading rubber processors in Thailand and Africa. Soon, my career will come full circle, as I find myself once again involved in the management of a global rubber company, in close proximity to rubber smallholders.

My dream is that R1, under the stewardship of HRG, can be a smallholder-centric company, an achievement that would be a real success and a legacy to treasure. The new group has the power to contribute to *all* stakeholders within the industry, changing the lives of smallholders and being a valuable part of the communities and nations in which we operate. This is the legacy I look forward to leaving.

Acknowledgments

I believe that we are who we are largely due to God's blessing, the people who have touched us, and our varied experiences in this journey of life. I am truly blessed in many ways and eternally grateful for the love and generosity of many people in my life. Much as I would like to, I may not succeed in acknowledging them all. However, I would like to mention a few significant persons who have inspired me, helped me, and positively influenced the course of my life.

AN ACKNOWLEDGMENT TO FAMILY

Firstly, I owe eternal gratitude to my parents, my late dad, Sinaya Anthony, and mum, Mary Sesudasan, for their boundless love and many sacrifices, for instilling in me values and virtue, and for preparing their firstborn to have a chance of achieving all-around success in life. I treasure my dad's humility, his generosity, his hard work and positive outlook even in the face of the most difficult circumstances. He always placed the interests of others ahead of his own. It was the same with my sisters, Anna, Jacintha, Philomena, and Shirley, and my brother, Mike (now the Reverend Father Michael Dass). It is a special blessing to have a supporting and loving family.

AN ACKNOWLEDGMENT TO TEACHERS AND SPIRITUAL DIRECTORS

While attending school at St. Michael's Institution in Ipoh, Malaysia, I was fortunate enough to be guided by caring teachers who took a great interest in my personal and academic development. In particular, I am eternally indebted to two Lasallian brothers, Brother Casimir Hannon and Brother Ultan Paul, who coached me in the school debating team and school plays. They instilled in me a strong sense of self-belief and a can-do spirit that formed the foundations of my leadership abilities.

Growing up, I benefited from several exemplary French Catholic spiritual advisors based in Ipoh, my hometown: the Reverend Father Rigottier, the Reverend Father Lucian Catel, and the Reverend Father Emile Grandgirard. Their selfless care and dedication to the less fortunate people in their midst firmly planted the desire to do good in my young heart.

AN ACKNOWLEDGMENT TO FRIENDS

I value good friends in life. They are angels sent by God, guarding and guiding me to flourish and find happiness. I thank God for giving me some exceptional friends. My best friend and confidant since childhood is Leo Antoni, a true friend in need and deed. Somehow, he is always there when I'm in need of his counsel to raise me up. Other friends who have cheered me are my mates from Xavier Hall, where I boarded when I was at university. My roommate Tee Boo and hostel mates Hardeep, Noel John, Sunny Lee, Moi Fong, Keng Lun, Tony Chang, Raghbir, Lee S. C., and Y. K. Lee have remained steadfast friends for more than forty-five years. I am also indebted to Louis Doss, my close friend from school. Friends add meaning to a fulfilling life.

AN ACKNOWLEDGMENT TO MENTORS

Over the past forty years of my career, some very special people have been the thrust and wind beneath my wings, helping me soar higher and higher. I am especially indebted to John Morris, Tan Sri Dr. B. C. Sekhar, Dato Suleiman Manan, Tun Lim Keng Yaik, Tan Sri Syed Jabbar, J. C. Rajarao, Jeral De Souza, Munir Hassan, Dr.

Pongsak Kerdvongbundit, and Oei Hong Bie. A special acknowledgment is due to my soulmate from MARDEC days, Dato Dr. Mahmood Kadir. We made a great team, supporting one another for the glory of MARDEC. All of these people have inspired me and mentored me toward my true potential. I am forever thankful to them for being an important part of my life journey when it mattered.

AN ACKNOWLEDGMENT TO MY WORK TEAM

I must acknowledge my team leaders at R1, who have stood by me and contributed significantly to making the R1 dream come true. Special thanks to Ng Meng Chew, Lim K. H., V. S. Maniam, Syed Noh, Benson Lim, Casey Oh, William Ho, Ling C. Y., Thirunavukkarasu, Leow W. C., Toshinobu Handa, Richard Stauffer, Thad Goff, T. C. Ong, Kennie Lee, Thao, Vinay, Keith Lim, Yeoh W. C., Leslie Cheng, Sastry Srinivas, Pek T.Y., Stephen Evans, and Frans DeJong. I owe deep gratitude to Jennifer Ho, my assistant in Malaysia for more than thirty years. She has enough firsthand knowledge and capability to write this book herself. I am also thankful to Anderline Ea, my assistant in Singapore, for her sincere support in my work.

AN ACKNOWLEDGMENT TO MY SHAREHOLDERS

I am honored and thankful to the board of directors of R1, and to the shareholders of MARDEC Bhd, Cargill

Asia Pacific Ltd, Thaveesak Holding Co (VB), Kian Inn, Hainan State Farms Investment Ltd, and Hainan Rubber Group Ltd for their confidence, trust, and responsibility to lead R1 Group.

AN ACKNOWLEDGMENT TO MY PUBLISHERS

I thank my publishing team: John Vercher, Rob Wolf Petersen, and Barbara Boyd for their excellent work bringing my book to life.

AN ACKNOWLEDGMENT TO MY WIFE AND SONS

I am deeply grateful to my wife, Anne Debra, and sons, Joshua Harsha and Juleon Toshan, for their endless understanding and patience, and for encouraging me to pursue my passion.

AN ACKNOWLEDGMENT TO GOD

Mostly, I am ever thankful to the Almighty for all blessings, for the opportunities in my life, for providing me with all I need, and for guiding me to a life of purpose, meaning, and fulfillment. All praise be His.

About the Author

SANDANA DASS joined the rubber industry in 1973 as a "rubber scholar" with the Malaysian Rubber Fund Board, a position that led him to a twenty-eight-year association with MARDEC, the Malaysian Rubber Development Company. In 2001, Sandana founded R1 International and became its group managing director and CEO. He oversees R1's global operations in nine countries and shares his forty-plus years of experience by acting as an expert advisor on rubber trade and marketing to the government and trade associations. Sandana Dass has an honors degree in economics and a master's in entrepreneurship.

www.ingramcontent.com/pod-product-compliance
Lightning Source LLC
Chambersburg PA
CBHW031934190326
41519CB00007B/535